Denis MacShane is a professional journalist who has
worked on the *Daily Mirror* and BBC television and
radio. He is also a journalist's journalist, having been
on the executive of the National Union of
Journalists since 1974, and its President in 1978–79.

Using the Media is one of a series of Workers'
Handbooks for trade unionists. The series includes
Patrick Kinnersly's *The Hazards of Work*, a workers'
guide to health and safety; Christopher Hird's *Your
Employers' Profits*, on company accounts; and Jeremy
McMullen's *Rights at Work*, a workers' guide to
employment law. Handbooks in preparation cover
women workers; workers' participation; negotiating
with management; young workers; fringe benefits;
payment systems.

First published 1979 by Pluto Press Limited
Unit 10 Spencer Court, 7 Chalcot Road, London NW1 8LH

Copyright © Pluto Press 1979

ISBN 0 86104 089 9 paperback
      0 86104 090 2 hardback

Designed by John Finn
Cover designed by Colin Bailey

Set, printed and bound in Great Britain by
Cox & Wyman Ltd, Reading

Denis MacShane

Using the Media

**How to deal with the press,
television
and radio**

Pluto Press

Contents

Acknowledgements

This book has grown out of the TUC course on 'Using the Media'. I have drawn freely on the ideas of Doug Gowan, David Kerrigan, Bill Brett, John Tulloch and Noel Howell, who have worked regularly on the course. They have my thanks.

I should also like to thank Carol Barnes, Francis Beckett, John Creaby, Jonathan Dimbleby, Christopher Hird, Mike Kidron, Anne Lamming, Jeremy McMullen, John Perkins and Alan Pike, who read all or sections of the different drafts of the book and whose suggestions and advice have been invaluable.

I am grateful to the Press Association and the *Camden Journal*, for their help, and to Ronnie Kelly for permission to use the drawing on page 132, which first appeared in the *New Statesman*.

As a journalist, trade-union and political activist and TUC tutor I have discussed with countless workers the problems of using the media. I hope I have answered some of the questions they have raised.

1.

Introduction

This handbook is designed to equip:

- workers
- trade-union officials
- community activists
- local political activists
- pressure groups

for the most effective use of the media. But it needs to be said from the outset that, even if every single technique mentioned in the book is deployed to maximum effect, it cannot *guarantee* favourable or even fair treatment.

The British mass media is firmly locked into (or, in the BBC's case, linked to) British capitalism. In the first place, there are all the implications of formal ownership (see Chapter 3). Secondly, although fringe radicalism may sometimes be tolerated, the career structure of journalism puts a premium on **conformity** to economic and social norms. Thirdly, and just as important, there are established **news values** (see Chapter 4), which emphasise the sensational, the confrontations, the personal, at the expense of proper analysis.

At key moments, the whole weight of the mass media can be thrown against working people. One such moment was the industrial crisis of early 1979, when hundreds of thousands of workers, fed up with years of pay restraint, asserted their right to a living wage. The press reaction was hysterical. The *Sun*, for example, announced that three millions would be laid off because of the lorry drivers' strike – in fact the figure never exceeded 200,000. A picket was killed by a lorry driven by a blackleg and the newspapers relegated the story to an inside page – compare that with media treatment of injuries received by policemen during the Grunwick mass picketing.

When the IRA blew up an oil storage depot on Canvey Island, the usually sensible *Evening Standard* produced this editorial:

Last night's explosions at Canvey Island oil storage depot
and at a gasometer in East Greenwich are the IRA's style
of secondary picketing.

Like the lorry drivers' roving interference squads these
political vandals roam in well-drilled cadres, bent on harm-
ing the livelihoods and lowering the spirits of innocent
victims.

Such hysterical hatred against working people and their
basic trade-union rights cannot be fundamentally changed while
current patterns of ownership and journalistic operation continue. For the time being, and therefore in this book, we have to
take the media – the newspapers, the magazines, television and
radio – as they are. But this does not mean leaving them to get
on with it. Our basic argument is that the media have a way of
operating which should hold no fear or mystery for non-
professionals.

Workers and others have a duty to ensure that no barrier
is put between their case and its public presentation in the media
on account of lack of knowledge of how news is produced or
undue wariness about the behaviour of journalists. Newspapers
and broadcasting stations are not neutral. They use people. But
they can also be used.

Employers, both private and public, have long since learned
how to use the media. There are an estimated 10,000 full- or
part-time Public Relations Officers (PROs) working for British
industry and commerce, whose job is to make sure that the
employer's case is put over effectively. The government has 1,900
PROs doing a similar job in Whitehall. Inside the BBC, which
employs 25,000 workers, such is the importance attached to good
public relations that the chief PRO is on a more senior grade
than the editor of BBC Television News.

For most workers, their families and friends, the press, TV
and radio are the chief source of information about what is
happening. The socialist, community and trade-union press
circulates to activists; but, for most people, news about trade
unions, community or single-issue campaigns, political activity
generally is available only in the mainstream media. Even if
workers distrust what they read in the newspapers or see on
television, there is no other easy way they can check facts and
compare opinions about events outside their immediate circle.

Dealing with the media can mean doing unnatural things.
Although suspicion is justified and a watchful attitude always

necessary, it is essential to try to make personal and **friendly contact** with journalists. A trade-union official will have to give a home phone-number to journalists – something which may be kept a close secret from colleagues and members – and yet it is that home phone-number which may make all the difference between a favourable and an unfavourable story being published.

The business of journalism and dealing with journalists is a breeding ground for cynicism. But journalists themselves – many of them from family and educational backgrounds with no understanding of trade unionism – will only be confirmed in newsroom stereotypes of shop stewards and branch secretaries if they meet surly, uncooperative responses. Many journalists are badly paid trade unionists themselves (see Chapter 3); many of them want to see their newspapers or television programmes used to expose 'the unacceptable face of capitalism' or to challenge arbitrary authority. Those journalists need help and encouragement, not a hostile brush-off.

Here is just one example of how a news story can be used to get the public on the workers' side:

In 1974, Midlands building contractors wanted to introduce the regular use of a new and very heavy brick, weighing considerably more than the traditional brick. Building workers objected and called a press conference. Reporters were invited to try carrying a hod full of the new bricks up a ladder. They all collapsed before putting a foot on the first rung. UCATT arranged for some members who had suffered severe muscle strain from carrying the new bricks to be available for interview. These interviews, combined with the reporters' own accounts, produced stories which were firmly on the workers' side.

Most of the examples in this handbook are to do with workers and their unions; but the techniques suggested are essentially neutral. They can be used by any groups or individuals who have a case to put over and want to do the best possible for that case in presenting it to the media.

News media are of vital importance, both for workers and for anyone actively promoting changes in society. To a certain extent, they are there to be used. This book tries to show how.

2.

How to use this book

Initiating and reacting to press coverage /
negotiations / disputes / campaigns / union
affairs / consumer affairs / going to a tribunal
/ becoming an expert / political issues /
general use of the media

This handbook covers the whole spectrum of relations
between workers and the media. It can be read as a whole, or
particular chapters can be referred to in appropriate situations.

The worker who finds him/herself suddenly asked to take
part in a **television studio discussion** should turn to Chapter 9
(which looks at television interviews in general) and to pages
135–51 in particular, which examine some of the fine points of
studio interviews.

A regional trade-union officer will want to build up a
relationship with all the media in his or her area systematically.
He or she should work through the whole book, paying particular attention to Chapter 8 on **making contact**.

Initiating and reacting to press coverage

Sometimes you want to **initiate** press or broadcasting
coverage, sometimes to **react** to what has already appeared in
the newspapers or to inquiries from journalists.

Initiating press coverage is covered in Chapters 5–7 on
press releases, pictures and **news conferences**, and in Chapter 11
on **access programmes and columns**. It is also important to know
how you can tell journalists, *in advance of* a newsworthy event,
when and where it will happen – but in such a way that the
impact of the event is not spoiled:

In August 1978 two political protests were made in London.
The Right to Work campaign occupied the Tory Headquarters
in Smith Square in protest at a cynical advertising campaign.

At the same time, community activists in East London, led by the local Communist Party, occupied a drawbridge which allowed yachts in and out of the exclusive yacht basin in St Katherine's dock. The Right to Work action got much wider coverage than the yacht protest. The reason? The Right to Work organisers told many more journalists and photographers in advance. The Communist Party told only a few journalists, and would not provide details about the yacht protest over the telephone.

In fact, as the section on embargoes in Chapter 5 (on press releases) shows, you can give journalists information in advance and they will respect the confidentiality of that information until the time you want it released.

As for reacting, anyone in an elected-representative position, from the rawest shop steward upwards, has to face the probability of a phone-call from a reporter trying to find out what is going on or asking for a comment on an already publicised situation. Chapter 8, on what to say to journalists, explains the techniques reporters use to get the information *they* want you to give them rather than the facts and point of view *you* ought to put over.

Chapter 12, on complaints, covers the most effective ways to protest or gain redress from the media when a wrong or biased report appears. However, the purpose of complaining is not just to extract revenge in a particular case: journalists should be under constant pressure to be fair.

Negotiations

The media can be extremely helpful during a negotiation. In most large industries, workers deal with one section of the management (the personnel or industrial-relations department) and perhaps the most senior manager (the Managing Director). Often other managers do not know negotiations are taking place.

If you explain the details of the claim in the media – stressing the company's ability to pay, and indicating the consequences of a failure to settle – you can convey the strength and determination of the union's position to sections of management other than the representatives you meet in face-to-face negotiation.

As for shareholders, their understanding of your case may depend entirely on media coverage of the negotiation.

Your own members and colleagues also read newspapers and/or watch television. With an authoritative and confident statement you can increase their confidence in the union's position during negotiation:

> The 1977 claim for Ford workers presented by the TGWU was released to the press. It was published in the form of a pamphlet full of detailed research on the claim and showing how Ford's profits made full settlement possible. Labour correspondents wrote about how impressive it was and its publication gave the union a commanding position at the start of the negotiations.

Amongst small firms, a dispute in any one of them can have serious knock-on effects for others in the area. Employers' unity tends to buckle under the pressure of lost income and disappearing profits. If employers read in the media that negotiations somewhere else are breaking down, and that a dispute may develop that could endanger continuity of output or service upon which their *own* firms depend, they may lean on the obstinate employer and tell him to be more conciliatory. But unless they hear about the negotiation difficulties through the media, they will not know that they should begin exerting pressure.

If you decide to use the media in negotiations, work out carefully what will be said. Avoid the unquotable style of some workers' spokespersons – 'We are continuing to negotiate at this present moment in time and that is all I can say', etc. (see Chapters 8 and 9).

Disputes

Workers struggling against their employers are not the only ones who get involved in disputes. There are also the struggles of, for example:

- tenants against landlords
- community health councils against health authorities
- councillors against Whitehall directives
- anti-racists against fascist politicians
- parents wanting more nurseries against local councils
- shoppers against supermarket chains
- local communities against road builders

All these groups, involved in different kinds of disputes, can find themselves the object of media attention. Chairpersons, secretaries, convenors, councillors should all read the sections in Chapter 8 on **how to deal with journalists' inquiries.**

In many cases, your opponent (be it employer, landlord, local authority, government) will not want **publicity**, and you may gain advantage merely by threatening to produce it.

If the dispute attracts media attention it is important to seize the initiative and get your point of view over to journalists.

As well as putting out a press release (Chapter 5), you should consider organising members and their families to write letters to the local papers, or take part in **phone-ins** (Chapter 11).

A little thought can produce amusing ways of putting over your side in a dispute:

> In 1977, Rolls-Royce car-division engineers were in dispute with their local management. They decided to write to the the Queen apologising because a new Rolls-Royce promised for her Jubilee Year would be delivered late as a result of the industrial action they were forced to take in pursuit of their claim. They telephoned the *Guardian*'s Labour Editor and gave him the details. The resulting story increased pressure on the management.

Campaigns

Campaigns are **close to the heart of** union branches, tenants groups and local political organisations. There are **negative** campaigns – against a factory closure, a hospital closure, the re-routing of a bus route – and there are **positive** campaigns – for a new nursery school, better safety conditions, an increase in internal union democracy.

A campaign needs planning and some long-term commitment, and you can use the whole battery of media weapons in launching and running it.

Launch your campaign at a **news conference** (Chapter 7). Apart from preparing press releases, think up some ways in which the campaign can be put over visually. If you organise a demonstration or hand in a petition, make sure the media know about the chances of getting good **pictures** or film (Chapter 6).

If as part of your campaign you want to expose some scandal, or if there is a particular case (for example, of poor safety conditions in a factory) which would make a good television film for programmes like *World In Action*, then send a letter and a report to the producer and follow it up with phone-calls and a visit (Chapter 9).

Union affairs

The local media (weekly newspapers in particular) like to publish details of ordinary humdrum comings and goings. So if senior officials are making a visit, let the local press know (but do ask the officials first). Tell the press about new appointments or elections or any special issues that the branch or trades council is taking up.

Any achievements by local trade unionists can be reported to the local media (see the section on **good news**, in Chapter 4). In its excellent *Union Stewards' Handbook*, COHSE, the National Health Service union, has a useful section on handling the media, which concludes:

> Remember always the underlying purpose of the press as far as you are concerned, namely to promote the union, its membership and policies.

Consumer affairs

Workers are in a unique position to blow the whistle on cheating by companies who sell goods or services to the public.

If a branch feels that a price rise or some diminution of service announced by their employer is unfair or not justified, they should consider making their concern public. In 1976 the Nottingham district office of the Tobacco Workers Union issued a press release about a rise in cigarette prices:

> John Player and Sons cigarette price rises announced to take place from 1 November have led to a 'jumping of the gun' by some shopkeepers.
>
> Members of the Tobacco Workers' Union in the John Player factories are gravely concerned about this form of profiteering.
>
> Large amounts of Players cigarettes are held by wholesalers and some shops. These cigarettes would have been bought at the pre-1 November price.
>
> Mr Graham Ferris, a member of the union said, 'The speed with which the increase has been passed on to the public was nothing short of daylight robbery.'
>
> The Tobacco Workers' Union have asked the company repeatedly to put a date of manufacture on tobacco products to avoid this form of profiteering.

Trade unionists and their relatives are consumers too. They share with the rest of their fellows an interest in keeping prices as low as possible and in maintaining public services which central and local government want to cut:

> In summer 1978, London bus crews went on strike against a £8,000,000 cut in services proposed by the GLC. The busmen's convenor said 'London Transport can expect more strikes of this type if they don't think again. These cuts will reduce services, they'll reduce people's wages and they'll enrage the public. We have people waiting for up to an hour and a half for a bus at the moment. With what they're planning it will be worse.'

Going to a tribunal

Industrial tribunals, especially those hearing unfair dismissal cases, are now an excellent way of exposing employers' bad practices through the media. **Journalists** have full access to these tribunals and **should be tipped off** (see pages 81ff.) beforehand if an interesting case is due to be heard. An advance press release can be issued (see page 88) explaining why the tribunal hearing is considered important. Equal-pay or race-discrimination cases heard by tribunals should also be brought to journalists' notice. After a tribunal hearing which has commanded news interest, it may be worthwhile calling a news conference (see Chapter 7) at which the persons going through the tribunal as well as their representatives can comment on its outcome.

Becoming an expert

Television and radio like experts and pundits – individuals who can comment generally on current issues. Too often they are academics or full-time politicians, often based in London. There is no reason why a trade-union representative, lay or full-time, should be restricted to just his or her own union's affairs. On the economy, industrial relations, national politics, the Common Market, foreign affairs there is every reason why the worker's voice should be heard in the studio. **Local TV and radio producers need to be told** (see page 138) **that you are available to comment.**

> A Northern Area organiser for APEX, who mentioned casually after a hard-news interview on Tyne Tees Television that he was involved in some interesting sex-discrimination cases, found himself invited on

to a midafternoon women's programme to talk generally about the
subject.

Political issues

Political parties or bodies campaigning on specific issues
need no prompting to take up general political matters –
unemployment, racism and fascism, wage control, Tory policies
generally, anti-union legislation, nuclear weapons, human rights.

Trade-union branches and trades councils active in these
fields too should let the media know what is happening. The
following report appeared in the anti-fascist journal, *Searchlight*,
and was based on a local newspaper cutting sent in from Yorkshire:

> In 1978 trade unionists in Huddersfield held a special
> meeting to discuss Kirklees Council's policy of hiring out
> public buildings to the National Front. Trade unionists,
> representatives of the churches and other groups who were
> at the meeting decided to ask the Mayor of Kirklees to
> receive a delegation from the Trades Council, and recom-
> mended that the Trades Council should form a broad-based
> committee to combat racism.

Not all press releases or handed-in reports will appear in
the local paper. Even professional PROs think that a success rate
of one story printed for every two or three press releases sent out
is a good one. But socialist groups and trade-union organisations should always send an account of their activities to the
left-wing press and to trade-union journals (see Chapter 3, and
the Appendix for addresses). These papers are always anxious
for material (or 'copy', as it is known in the trade) and for news
presented professionally in the form of press releases.

General use of the media

The examples listed above are the clearest and most
obvious uses of the media. Stories about such trade-union or
local-community activity can be found in nearly every newspaper
every day. Yet journalists have often had to extract the details
from trade unionists or political activists, who were unwilling or
too nervous to approach reporters themselves.

It is better by far to decide to use the media and present

yourself to *them* – to go on the **offensive** as it were. That way you can **increase coverage** of your work, and at the same time **communicate it to a wider constituency than your immediate colleagues.** Seize the initiative, and ensure that journalists know the facts and opinions from your point of view.

To do this successfully you have to be more than a desiccated duplicating machine churning out press releases. You have to build a relationship (see Chapter 8), so that journalists will trust what you say and, as they become more confident of their relationship with you, will turn to you as a reliable source of news and comment in your sphere of activity.

3.

The media

Newspapers / television / radio / local news
agencies and freelances / magazines, journals
and the left press / teletext / ownership /
unions in the media

Newspapers

The national press

Fourteen million copies of the eight national dailies are
sold every day, and it is reckoned that an average of three people
will read every copy sold. So when all the papers carry the same
story and give it roughly the same treatment (for example, a
statement by the Prime Minister attacking a particular strike)
the effect can be overwhelming.

**Table 1: Circulation of Fleet Street
newspapers in the first half of 1978***

Sun	3,930,554
Daily Mirror	3,778,038
Daily Express	2,400,907
Daily Mail	1,932,808
Daily Telegraph	1,344,968
The Times	293,989
Guardian	273,201
Financial Times	180,793

* A new national newspaper, the *Daily Star*, was launched in Manchester
in November 1978. It began printing in Fleet Street in 1979 and by June
1979 had reached a circulation of 1,011,116 – an impressive achievement
which probably owed much to its low cover price, 6p. Although
owned by the right-wing chairman of Express Newspapers, Victor
Matthews, and shamelessly sexist and sensational, many of its editorials
were sympathetic to low-paid workers.

The suspension of *The Times* and *Sunday Times* in November 1978
pushed up the circulation of other quality newspapers in 1979.

Circulation and readership figures can, however, be a misleading guide to the real influence of different newspapers. In 1976, at the end of the TUC Congress, the President of the TUC, Cyril Plant, neatly summed up the different readerships of the national newspapers:

■ *The Times*: read by the people who run the country

■ *Daily Mirror*: read by the people who think they run the country

■ *Guardian*: read by the people who think they ought to run the country

■ *Morning Star*: read by the people who think the country ought to be run by another country

■ *Daily Mail*: read by the wives of the people who run the country

■ *Financial Times*: read by the people who own the country

■ *Daily Express*: read by the people who think the country ought to be run as it used to be run

■ *Daily Telegraph*: read by the people who still think it is

■ and then, of course, the readers of the *Sun* – they don't care who runs the country as long as she has big tits!

More seriously, the classification of readership of the national press according to social grade (see profile) shows the importance of separating out the national newspapers not only according to size of readership, but according to the influence and power of those readers.

The **social grades** into which newspaper readers are divided were originally for the use of government statisticians, but since the development of advertising they have been used chiefly by advertising agencies as a means of indicating the purchasing power of the different readerships.

The grades are:

■ A – senior administrative and managers
■ B – middle managers, professional people
■ C1 – senior clerical, supervisory staff
■ C2 – skilled craftsworkers
■ D – semi- and unskilled workers
■ E – casual labourers.

Table 2: National newspaper readership profile 1978

		A	B	C1	C2	D	E
% of population over age 15		3	13	22	32	21	9
	Readership						
Sun	12,267,000	1	5	17	41	29	7
Daily Mirror	11,841,000	1	6	17	39	29	7
Daily Express	6,735,000	3	15	29	30	18	7
Daily Mail	5,465,000	4	16	31	28	15	6
Daily Telegraph	3,171,000	13	37	30	13	6	2
The Times	925,000	18	34	28	12	6	2
Guardian	861,000	9	41	30	14	6	1
Financial Times	707,000	16	36	33	9	5	1

If you want to get through to the people with the most authority and power in Britain, you should aim for *The Times*, the *Telegraph* and *Financial Times*. But **if you want to influence full-time officials in the trade-union movement,** you should concentrate on the *Guardian* (which has the second lowest circulation of any Fleet Street paper). Look at the pattern of trade-union officials' reading habits (this is based on a survey of trade-union officials who have passed through the TUC training course on using the media).

Table 3: The reading pattern of
trade union officials*

Guardian	65%
Daily Mirror	45
Morning Star	35
The Times	30
Sun	25
Daily Telegraph	20
Financial Times	15
Daily Express	10
Daily Mail	10

* Some officials regularly read more than
one newspaper, so percentages go over
100.

Even more significant is the large number of trade-union full-timers who read the *Morning Star* which, with its tiny circulation of 22,000, does not normally feature on the lists of mainstream national newspapers. In terms of communicating with influential activists in the trade-union movement, the *Morning Star* can be very significant. The General and Municipal Workers' Union officially pays for only two papers for each of its officials – the *Financial Times* and the *Morning Star*.

The weekly *Socialist Worker*, when it reached a circulation of 30,000 in the dying days of the 1970–74 Heath administration, had an influence amongst young, highly militant and politically conscious workers that probably exceeded the pro-Tory effect that a newspaper like the *Daily Express* had with the same group – even though the overall circulation of the *Daily Express* is a hundred times higher.

With the exception of the *Sun, The Times* and the *Financial Times*, all the national newspapers are printed in Manchester as well as in Fleet Street. The *Sun*, with only a London newsroom, has 150 journalists; the *Daily Mirror*, with newsrooms – and widely differing editions – in both London and Manchester, has nearly 500 journalists.

The national press is divided into the **quality press** – *The Times, Financial Times, Guardian* and *Daily Telegraph* – and the **popular press** – the rest.

The quality national papers print much more news from trade unions. *The Times*, the *Guardian*, the *Financial Times* and the *Daily Telegraph* have at least three reporters who specialise in trade-union news and nothing else.

Table 4: Circulation of national
Sunday newspapers 1978

News of the World	4,934,532
Sunday People	3,853,561
Sunday Mirror	3,832,394
Sunday Express	3,242,777
Sunday Times	1,409,296
Sunday Telegraph	844,589
Observer	688,458

The national Sunday newspapers show a similar gap between **mass readership** and **influential readership**.

Table 5: Sunday newspaper readership profile 1978

		A	B	C1	C2	D	E
% of population over age 15		3	13	22	32	21	9
	Readership	%					
News of the World	13,297,000	1	5	16	40	39	9
Sunday Mirror	12,149,000	1	7	20	40	26	6
Sunday People	11,304,000	1	7	19	39	27	8
Sunday Express	8,582,000	5	21	32	24	12	5
Sunday Times	3,777,000	13	33	31	15	7	2
Sunday Telegraph	2,500,000	11	31	32	16	7	2
Observer	2,282,000	9	32	31	17	8	3

The regional press

More than two-thirds of the provincial press, including weekly papers, is owned by just four firms: Westminster Press, Thomson Regional Newspapers, Associated Newspapers and United Newspapers (see page 40).

Most big towns have an evening paper appearing six nights a week.

Table 6: Number of evening newspapers

England	69
Scotland	5
Wales	4
N. Ireland	2
Eire	3
Guernsey	1
Jersey	1

All evening papers outside London have a monopoly. Consequently they have considerable penetration. In Manchester, for example, with its population of 950,000, the *Manchester Evening News* is read by as many as 815,000 people.* (The

* The Greater Manchester conurbation has a population of 2·8 million, but evening papers from Oldham, Bolton and Wigan also circulate in Greater Manchester.

readership profiles relate to the popular rather than the quality papers.)

Table 7: Evening newspaper readership profile 1978

		A	B	C1	C2	D	E
% of population over age 15		3	13	22	32	21	9
	Readership	%					
Birmingham Evening Mail	825,000	3	10	24	35	21	7
Manchester Evening News	815,000	1	9	20	38	27	5
Wolverhampton Express & Star	672,000	3	11	14	45	17	9
Liverpool Echo	599,000	—	6	14	34	36	10
Leeds Evening Post	463,000	2	7	15	48	20	6

The following cities in England and Wales have morning daily newspapers:

- Birmingham — *Birmingham Post*
- Bristol — *Western Daily Press*
- Cardiff — *Western Mail*
- Darlington — *Northern Echo*
- Ipswich — *East Anglian Daily Times*
- Leeds — *Yorkshire Post*
- Liverpool — *Liverpool Daily Post*
- Newcastle — *The Journal*
- Norwich — *Eastern Daily Press*
- Plymouth — *Western Morning News*
- Sheffield — *Morning Telegraph*

As you can see from the figures for Leeds and Birmingham, regional morning papers generally do not sell as well as their evening counterparts.

Table 8: **Circulation of morning and evening regional newspapers**

Leeds		
Yorkshire Post	morning	100,423
Evening Post	evening	184,377

Birmingham		
Birmingham Post	morning	45,080
Evening Mail	evening	341,259

Three factors have speeded up the decline of the morning regional press:

■ late night television news and early morning radio news, which have plenty of city or regional stories

■ more efficient distribution of Fleet Street papers

■ the rising cost of newspapers, which has cut into the habit of taking the regional morning paper as the second paper to the national daily.

Morning regional newspapers tend to have similar readership profiles to those of the *Daily Telegraph* and *The Times*.

There are three Sunday papers produced in the English provinces:

■ *Sunday Mercury*, produced in Birmingham and covering the West Midlands

■ *Sunday Sun*, produced in Newcastle for the North East

■ *Western Sunday Independent*, produced in Plymouth for Devon and Cornwall.

Scotland

The Scottish newspaper scene is a mixture of Fleet Street and provincial newspapers. Most of the Fleet Street dailies sell in Scotland, but there are three Scottish daily newspapers which circulate throughout the country.

Table 9: **Circulation of Scottish daily newspapers**

Daily Record Glasgow	720,000	(sister paper of *Daily Mirror*)
Glasgow Herald Glasgow	116,000	(similar readership profile to *Daily Telegraph*)
Scotsman Edinburgh	89,000	(similar readership profile to *The Times*)
Aberdeen Press and Journal	114,000	(circulates north of lowlands)

Scotland also has evening papers, produced in Glasgow, Greenock, Edinburgh, Aberdeen and Paisley. The *Sunday Mail* is produced in Glasgow. A giant publishing firm called D. C. Thomson,* based in Dundee, produces Scotland's biggest selling Sunday newspaper, *The Sunday Post*, as well as morning and evening papers in Dundee. Best known for the comics they produce, including the *Beano, Hotspur, Wizard* and *Dandy*, D. C. Thomson have resisted recognising trade unions since 1926. **Trade unionists should check with the print unions or the NUJ before contacting any D. C. Thomson newspaper.**

The weekly newspapers

Local weekly papers have a very different structure and rhythm from evening papers. They have much smaller staffs: for example, just nine journalists produce the North London weekly paper, the *Camden Journal*, compared with the seventy journalists producing the medium-sized *Coventry Evening Telegraph*.

Altogether there are one thousand weekly titles produced in Britain. However, the word 'title' is confusing. Very often it is the same paper being produced with a different front page and title according to where it is being sold.

There are about two hundred separate weekly newspaper newsrooms. A few weeklies come out two or three times a week (the *Southport Visitor*, for example, has a midweek edition).

Weekly papers need the raw material of news more than any other news media. They cannot rely on big national and foreign stories to fill up their pages. The journalists on a weekly paper are usually over-stretched and every week there is a hunt for local material. **If a story is presented to a local weekly paper**

* D. C. Thomson has no connection with the Thomson Organisation which owns *The Times, Sunday Times* and a chain of regional newspapers (see page 40ff. on ownership).

already written out as a news story, or statement, or speech, or press release (see Chapter 5), it will almost certainly be used.

> In 1978 the *Long Eaton Advertiser* was produced by a staff of five – editor, an 80-year-old sub-editor, and three juniors (see page 44ff.). One of the juniors said: 'Anything that comes in locally and is already written up as a story goes straight into the paper.'

To many people, the local weekly paper is a bit of a joke – the 'rag', not much better than a parish-pump magazine and badly lacking serious political and trade-union news and views. This attitude is mistaken. **Local weeklies are important:**

  ■ they tend to be read over a longer period of time and are left lying around

  ■ they are more carefully read and absorbed because they are usually bought on Saturday, a leisure day

  ■ they relate as directly as it is possible to the immediate life of the people in the circulation area.

The reason why many do not cover trade-union and political news, except superficially, is partly that such news is thought 'boring' – although the opposite is true in the national media where industrial and political reports dominate the news – and partly that local trade-union activists, tenants' groups and others have not worked at providing that news and being helpful and available to weekly newspaper journalists.

The Press Association

There is only one national news agency in Britain, the Press Association. The PA, as it is generally known, is owned on a cooperative basis by the provincial newspaper groups.

The PA provides a continual stream of news stories on a telex machine to each provincial newspaper in Britain and Ireland as well as to all the national newspaper and broadcasting newsrooms in London. Two hundred and fifty journalists work in shifts, 24 hours a day, seven days a week, to produce a daily total of 220,000 words.

As well as news organisations, institutions like parliament, government ministries, embassies and big firms subscribe to the PA. Most provincial newspapers rely heavily on it for news outside their region, particularly trade-union news:

> On the first day of the NUJ provincial newspaper strike in December 1978, the first seven paragraphs of the report on the strike in the Leeds-produced *Yorkshire Post* were identical to

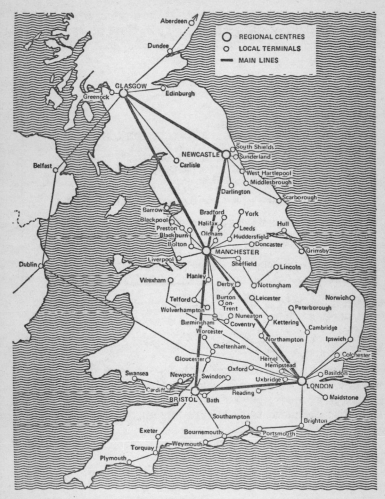

PA's distribution network in Britain

those in the *Sheffield Morning Telegraph*. Both papers had taken the story from the PA and used it without further inquiry or re-writing.

If you can get a story on to the PA, every important newsroom in the country will read it. It is therefore always worth sending them a copy of a statement or a press release, even if you do not send it to other national newsrooms.

```
PA
TODAY'S DAIRY
 WEDNESDAY, JANUARY 24, 1979 ·
 0900 LONDON: NATIONAL FARMERS' UNION CONFERENCE CONTINUES,
 CENTRAL HALL, WESTMINSTER (STAFF)
 1000 LONDON: TWO MEN APPEAR CHARGED WITH OFFENCES CONNECTED
 WITH OPEN KADET CAR SOUGHT BY POLICE AFTER CHRISTMAS BOMBINGS,
 BOW STREET MAGISTRATES (STAFF)
 1000 LONDON: TUC GENERAL COUNCIL, CONGRESS HOUSE (STAFF)
 1000 LONDON: LABOUR PARTY NATIONAL EXECUTIVE MEETS, TRANSPORT
 HOUSE (STAFF)
 1300 LONDON: METROPOLITAN POLICE COMMISSIONER SIR DAVID MCNEE
 AT PARLIAMENTARY PRESS GALLERY LUNCHEON, HOUSE OF COMMONS (STAFF)·
 1400 GLASGOW: PUBLIC SECTOR UNIONS MEET TO DECIDE ON PLANS FOR
 FUTURE INDUSTRIAL SECTION, GMWU OFFICES (STAFF)
 END 0800 24/1 TFD NNN TODAYS DIARY
```

An early schedule from the PA, giving a preliminary indication of the stories it will be covering.

Other news agencies

The PA is the only national news agency operating in Britain. The other agencies which are sometimes credited in newspaper stories – Reuters, AFP (Agence France Presse), UPI (United Press International) – are foreign news agencies providing a service of international news.

Reuters is based in Fleet Street and sends out news about British events to subscribers around the world.

Universal News Service (UNS, Gough Square, London EC4) is an expanding telex agency which sends out a mixture of news statements and press releases to a number of newsrooms. It operates as a quasi-public-relations agency, and large companies pay a fee to UNS to have their press releases sent out.

In order to maintain a high volume of output, UNS will normally put any press release with strong news value on its telex machine.

PA

STRIKES 1 RAIL
 TALKS IN LONDON AIMED AT SETTLING THE NATIONWIDE RAIL DISPUTE
BROKE DOWN YESTERDAY FOLLOWING A WALKOUT BY MR RAY BUCKTON, THE
GENERAL SECRETARY OF THE MILITANT TRAIN DRIVERS' UNION ASLEF.
 AND MR BUCKTON, WHO STORMED ANGRILY OUT OF THE MEETING BY BRITISH
RAIL WITH THE THREE UNIONS INVOLVED IN THE DISPUTE, SAID LATER
THAT THURSDAY'S ONE-DAY RAIL STRIKE - THE FOURTH IN TWO WEEKS
- WOULD GO AHEAD AS PLANNED.
 BEFORE LEAVING THE MEETING WITH THE UNION'S PRESIDENT, MR BILL
RONSKLEY, MR BUCKTON SAID THERE HAD BEEN ''A VERY SERIOUS TURN FOR
THE WORSE.''
 ''I AM RATHER DISGUSTED AT WHAT HAS HAPPENED IN THIS MEETING
AFTER WHAT HAPPENED LAST NIGHT,'' HE SAID.

 THIS WAS A REFERENCE TO THE INTERVENTION BY TUC GENERAL SECRETARY
MR LEN MURRAY, WHO CALLED THE LEADERS OF THE THREE RAIL UNIONS
TOGETHER AND PERSUADED THEM TO RESUME TALKS.
 HOWEVER MR BUCKTON DECLINED TO SAY WHY HE HAD WALKED OUT OF THE
MEETING.
 HE SAID HE WOULD SAY NOTHING UNTIL HE HAD SPOKEN BY TELEPHONE
TO MR MURRAY.
 MR SID WEIGHELL, THE GENERAL SECRETARY OF THE NATIONAL UNION
OF RAILWAYMEN, SAID THE WALKOUT CAME WHEN THE TALKS MOVED ONTO
THE QUESTION OF ASLEF'S DEMANDS FOR A TEN PERCENT RESPON-
SIBILITY PAYMENT.
 THE NUR HAS ARGUED THAT IF ASLEF DRIVERS RECEIVED SUCH A PAYMENT
THEN ALL RAILWAY STAFF SHOULD.
 MR WEIGHELL SAID ASLEF WANTED THE DEMAND TO GO BEFORE A WORKING
PARTY BUT THE NUR AND THE WHITE COLLAR UNION TSSA WHICH WAS ALSO
PRESENT AT YESTERDAY'S MEETING, SUGGESTED THAT THE CLAIM SHOULD
BE EXPLORED AT TALKS OF THE RAILWAY STAFFS NATIONAL COUNCIL.

 ''THAT DIDN'T SUIT THE TRAIN DRIVERS AND THEY GOT UP AND WENT
OUT IN A HURRY,'' MR WEIGHELL SAID.
 MR CLIFF ROSE, BRITISH RAIL'S BOARD MEMBER FOR INDUSTRIAL RELATIONS,
SAID HE THOUGHT MR BUCKTON'S PHRASE ''VERY SERIOUS TURN FOR THE
WORSE'' MEANT THAT HE WAS DISAPPOINTED AT THE PROGRESS MADE ON
HIS PRODUCTIVITY CLAIM.
 MR ROSE SAID HE WAS PROPOSING THAT THE THREE UNIONS MEET AGAIN
AT 11AM TODAY WITH PRIORITY BEING GIVEN TO THE DRIVERS'
RESPONSIBILITY PROPOSAL.
 MR WEIGHELL SAID THAT BOTH THE NUR AND THE TSSA WOULD BE PRESENT
AT THE MEETING, BUT IT IS UNLIKELY THAT ASLEF WILL ATTEND AS THE
UNION'S EXECUTIVE IS DUE TO MEET THEN TO DISCUSS THE SITUATION.
END 0430 24/1 RFH NNN STRIKES 3 RAIL

A typical PA industrial story sent out at 4.30 a.m. for use in
early editions of evening newspapers and for morning radio
news programmes.

Television

BBC Television News

There is a clear distinction between BBC TV News and BBC TV Current Affairs. The Television Newsroom produces:
- BBC-1 *Lunchtime News*
- BBC-1 *5.40 p.m. News*
- BBC-1 *Nine O'Clock News*

They also produce the news bulletins on BBC-2 and the short inserts into programmes like the old *Tonight** and *Grandstand*.

The eighty journalists in the BBC Television Newsroom have no connection with BBC current affairs output, which is responsible for programmes like *Panorama, Nationwide* and *The Money Programme*. In fact there is often a deadly rivalry between news and current affairs, and the newsroom keeps its reporters exclusively to work on news bulletins.

'We may all work for the BBC, but if you are a TV news reporter you probably feel closer to a reporter from the *Daily Telegraph* than one of your colleagues from *Nationwide*', is the way one seasoned news reporter described it.

The BBC-1 *Nine O'Clock News* has an audience of around 10 million.

Independent Television News

ITN is the mirror image of BBC TV News. There are three news bulletins broadcast daily each weekday:
- *News at One*
- *News at 5.45*
- *News At Ten*

All the words spoken in *News At Ten* would fill only about two and a half columns of a page in the *Guardian*. The problem for national TV news editors is not what to put in but what to leave out – they have the pick of the international and national stories each day to choose from.

Television Current Affairs

The main national-broadcasting current affairs programmes are the BBC's *Nationwide, Panorama* and *The Money*

* In 1979, BBC chiefs announced plans to axe *Tonight* and effect a closer working of news and current affairs operations with a joint programme going out nightly on BBC 2.

Programme and ITV's *TV Eye* (Thames Television), *World in Action* (Granada) and *Weekend World* (London Weekend Television).

The nightly programmes like *Nationwide* are in close touch with the BBC Newsroom, so will have a sense of the main daily events; but all the current affairs programmes like to discover their own exclusive material which can be shaped into a longer piece than would ever be used on a news bulletin.

If you watch the different programmes, it is easy to sense what kind of material they use for their items. *Weekend World* tends to be academic, *Nationwide* is more lightweight and is keen on off-beat human stories, and *World in Action* specialises in campaigning exposés.

> The South East Regional Council of the TUC contacted *Nationwide* about a polio victim who was suffering because the local health authority had cut back on her nursing care as part of the public expenditure cutbacks. A full dossier of letters between MPs, unions, the health authority and the DHSS was given to *Nationwide*. The film that was made did not dwell on the public expenditure cuts but showed an extremely courageous woman battling to lead a normal life. The ensuing public sympathy put pressure on the health authority, which restored some of the nursing service.

Regional television

All the regional centres in Britain have a television station which broadcasts regional news. Both the BBC and the ITV network put out half-hour programmes at 6 p.m. each weekday, consisting of film reports, news items and studio interviews about the day's events in the region and material of general interest from the region. These 6 p.m. programmes are produced and edited locally in the different centres.

There is no particular difference between BBC and ITV stations – their journalistic quality and interest in trade-union news varies according to the ability and predilections of the different programme producers and editors. Three of the BBC stations in the English regions – Manchester, Bristol and Birmingham – as well as the BBC TV Newsrooms in Cardiff, Glasgow and Belfast – have a specialist industrial correspondent. However, their brief is not simply trade-union news. Much of their time is spent on company news, reports on new products, and general economic news relevant to the region, such as export drives or import penetration.

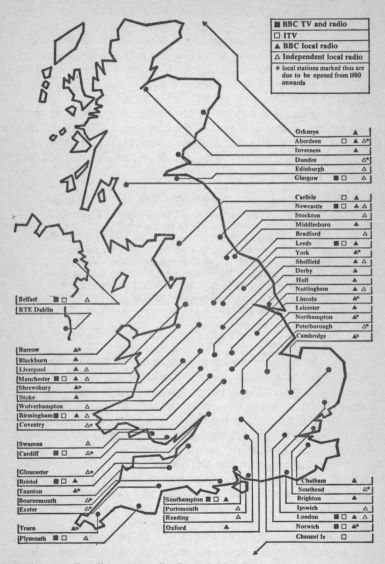

■ BBC TV and radio			
□ ITV			
▲ BBC local radio			
△ Independent local radio			
* local stations marked thus are due to be opened from 1980 onwards			

Orkneys		▲	
Aberdeen	□	▲	△*
Inverness		▲	
Dundee			△*
Edinburgh			△
Glasgow	■ □		△

Carlisle	□	▲	
Newcastle	■ □	▲	△
Stockton			△
Middlesboro		▲	
Bradford			△
Leeds	■ □	▲	
York		▲*	
Sheffield		▲	△
Derby		▲	
Hull		▲	
Nottingham		▲	△
Lincoln		▲*	
Leicester		▲	
Northampton		▲*	
Peterborough			△*
Cambridge		▲*	

Belfast	■ □		△
RTE Dublin			

Barrow		▲*	
Blackburn		▲	
Liverpool		▲	△
Manchester	■ □	▲	△
Shrewsbury		▲*	
Stoke		▲	
Wolverhampton			△
Birmingham	■ □	▲	△
Coventry			△*

Swansea			△
Cardiff	■ □		△*

Gloucester			△*
Bristol	■ □	▲	
Taunton		▲*	
Bournemouth			△*
Exeter			△*

Truro		▲*	
Plymouth	■ □		△

Southampton	■ □	▲	
Portsmouth			△
Reading			△
Oxford		▲	

Chatham		▲	
Southend			△*
Brighton		▲	
Ipswich			△
London	■ □	▲	△
Norwich	■ □	▲*	
Channel Is	□		

Television and radio stations in the British Isles

It is important to remember that the different parts of television journalism are produced by wholly separate teams. The journalists in the national BBC TV newsroom have no connection with their colleagues who produce *Nationwide*. Similarly, if *Granada Reports* covers a story in Stockport, there is no guarantee that ITN's Newsroom in London will hear about it.

Getting coverage

Getting coverage for your cause can have a powerful effect:

> A local campaign's best chance of getting on television is to plan a visual news story aimed at the box. The local footpath-protection group in Winslow, Buckinghamshire, were campaigning in 1972 to persuade the county council to replace a bridge on a footpath linking two villages. Press publicity and complaints to the council had no effect. So the group staged a double march of villagers from the two settlements converging on the site of the bridge. BBC Television were invited and they filmed the scene for the regional evening magazine programme. Three weeks later a new bridge was in position. (Christopher Hall, *How to Run a Pressure Group*, J. M. Dent. 1974.)

The usefulness of television for trade unions is well and truly matched by the usefulness of trade-union news to television. Industrial stories are vital to television news. Industrial news regularly takes up one-fifth of national TV news bulletins. The amount of time devoted to industrial stories is second only to national, political and foreign news. Senior correspondents are assigned to cover industrial news. ITN, for example, has had three specialist reporters permanently working on industrial news – a greater concentration of personnel than on any other subject except politics.

The Annan Committee, which spent the years 1974–77 examining the future of broadcasting, expressed concern about industrial reporting on television. It delivered this rebuke:

> (Industrial reporters and news editors) too often forget that to represent the management at their desks, apparently the calm and collected representatives of order, and to represent the shop stewards and picket lines stopping production, apparently the agents of disruption, gives a false

picture of what strikes are about. The broadcasters have fallen into the professional error of putting compelling camera work before news. Furthermore the causes of why people come out on strike are often extraordinarily complex. No reporter does his job adequately if he interviews only the leading shop steward or union official. The fact that a strike is not backed by a union does not exonerate broadcasters from discovering why the work force is out. The Glasgow Media Group reported that, in the unofficial Glasgow dustcart drivers' dispute in 1975, during 13 weeks and 21 interviews shown on the national news none of those on strike was interviewed. (*The Annan Report on the Future of Broadcasting*, London: HMSO 1977, Cmnd. 6753, p. 272)

For more detailed discussion of how to deal with television so that your case *is* heard, see Chapter 9.

Radio

BBC Radio News

BBC Radio News is the biggest single broadcasting operation in Britain. One hundred and fifty journalists work in shifts round the clock, 365 days a year in Broadcasting House to feed the appetite of the national radio networks for news.

The main bulletins are on Radio 4 at 7.00 and 8.00 a.m., at 1.00 p.m., at 6.00 p.m. and at 10.00 p.m.

As in television, the news bulletins and current affairs programmes are carefully **compartmentalised.** Listeners to BBC Radio 4 at 8.00 a.m. will hear the presenter say, 'Good morning, welcome to *Today* – and first the news from . . .' Another voice, that of the newsreader, then reads a news bulletin interspersed with short interviews and brief reports from reporters. The *Today* presenter comes in again at ten past eight and takes over for the rest of the programme.

The professionalism of the blending process leaves the impression that this is all one product. But, in fact, the news bulletin has been produced by the Newsroom, whereas the *Today* current-affairs production team is responsible for its own reports and interviews. That is why a big story handled one way in a news bulletin on radio may be followed a few minutes later in the current-affairs programme by a different reporter interviewing a different person about the same story in a different way.

The BBC Radio Newsroom produces the short headlines ('news on the hour every hour') on Radios 1 and 2 as well as the more grave, measured bulletins for Radio 3.

There is also a small unit in BBC Radio News which provides a service for the BBC's 20 local radio stations. Three times a day a sequence of interviews is sent out to all the BBC local radio stations; these consist of material of particular interest to individual local radio stations where the people involved have to be interviewed in London.

If, for example, some shop stewards travelled to London from Hull for a negotiation or to lobby parliament, it would be possible for a London-based BBC local radio interviewer to interview them and then send the interview to BBC Radio Humberside for the station's own use.

Independent Radio News

The Independent Radio Newsroom is situated just off Fleet Street. Its forty journalists provide a three-minute news bulletin every hour during the day.

Most of Britain's 19 commercial local radio stations use the IRN service, adding a couple of minutes of local news after the hourly national and international news has been read from London.

IRN operates from the same newsroom and shares some staff with LBC (London Broadcasting Company), which is the all-news, commercial radio station in London.

With only three minutes to fill, the IRN producers can barely manage to do more than give headlines to the main stories of the day. Although they only broadcast three minutes each hour, IRN has a teleprinter and an audio feed-line to each station and sends news and interviews along both which can then be used by the local station as it determines. However the IRN news producers tend to change their stories more than BBC radio newsmen and use more 20-second voice clips.

BBC Radio Current Affairs

Radio 4 is the principal channel for current affairs output. The main current-affairs 'slots' are:

▪ *Today*	6.30 a.m. to 8.35 p.m.
▪ *World at One*	1.00 p.m. to 1.40 p.m.
▪ *PM*	5.00 p.m. to 5.50 p.m.
▪ *World Tonight*	10.00 p.m. to 10.30 p.m.

There are also journalist-produced programmes like *Woman's Hour, You and Yours, Start the Week, Kaleidoscope*. These, while taking a softer or more highly specialised interest in certain topics, often cover the stories involving community activists or trade unionists.

Each programme has a separate production team headed by an editor with several producers working under him or her. Despite the BBC's resources, the producers who are charged with deciding what goes into these current affairs programmes – choosing who to interview, and so on – are often short of ideas that haven't appeared in other media.

There is no need to send the BBC Radio current-affairs programmes any routine material, but **do phone up producers if you have an unusual angle or an exclusive story.**

> In August 1977, ASTMS produced a guide to collective bargaining which was sent to 10,000 lay ASTMS representatives. Clive Jenkins talked to the BBC Radio 4 *Today* programme in advance and offered them an exclusive interview. In exchange for being interviewed, he promised the programme's deputy editor that he would not talk to other media until the *Today* interview had been broadcast. It is possible that *Today* would have interviewed Jenkins in any case, but the promise of exclusivity swung the balance.

As well as the formal current-affairs programmes on Radio 4, the BBC also transmits *Newsbeat* – a fast-moving news and current-affairs programme on Radio 1. *Newsbeat* is rather looked down upon by Radio 4 current-affairs producers because its interviews and reports are done in a snappy no-nonsense style. Radio 1's audience is ten times larger than Radio 4's, however, and has a higher proportion of working people listening.

The Jimmy Young Show, broadcast every morning on Radio 2, includes up to six interviews or current affairs spots. Senior politicians queue up to be interviewed by Jimmy Young, not because he is a soft interviewer – often he puts shrewder questions than Robin Day does – but because the Radio 2 audience is bigger and more socially diffuse than the Radio 4 audience. Producers on both *Newsbeat* and *The Jimmy Young Show* are always on the lookout for suggestions for interviews that are different from the more serious output of Radio 4.

Local radio

There are now 39 local radio stations in Britain, 20 BBC and 19 commercial. A further eighteen are to open after 1980.

Local radio newsrooms are always understaffed, because BBC and commercial local radio management dislike spending money on journalism. This can work to the trade unionist's advantage, because **the local radio journalist will be grateful for anyone who provides news in a pre-digested form.** Local radio newsrooms work very fast indeed. You can phone up with news of a walk-out and be on the air talking about it within minutes.

Most local radio stations do short bulletins every hour. These consist of seven or eight national and local stories written in a very crisp form. Even a big strike will only get 40 seconds – about 120 words or five paragraphs in the evening paper.

So **do not expect in-depth treatment on local radio.** The radio stations do not have enough staff to cover stories in depth, and the structure of the news output only allows superficial treatment.

Stations have slightly longer programmes in the early morning (6.00 to 9.00 a.m.), at midday (1.00 to 1.15 p.m.) and at teatime (between 6.00 and 6.30 p.m.), when the news stories are longer and more substantial interviews are broadcast. These interviews can be done over the telephone, but the sound quality is much better if they are recorded in the studio or on a tape-recorder. Because of the under-staffing problem in local radio you should always **offer to go to the studio** for an interview (if you can possibly fit it in), since this saves sending out a journalist to wherever you are.

Although the local radio stations do not have the staff to go out and find news, the news editor still has a lot of news flowing across the desk in the shape of agency stories, press releases, national stories from London and – one of the biggest sources of news for local radio – the stories that are published in the local newspapers. The news editors can therefore pick and choose what stories to run and, if they know that a particular story can include a spoken voice costing no newsroom time or money, they are more likely to be favourably inclined.

Local news agencies and freelances

All but the smallest towns have independent journalists who, on their own or in a small partnership, cover different stories and then sell them to different newsrooms.

For example, a freelance reporter may learn about a sacking that the union is going to fight over. The freelance will get the facts together, write up the story and telephone it to the local evening paper, the local radio stations, the local television newsrooms. If it is a particularly good story, the freelance will sell it to the Press Association or the national newspapers.

You can **short-circuit** contacting all the different newsrooms in a town or region by getting in touch with the local freelance or news agency about your story. If it's newsworthy, it will be 'sold' to all the newsrooms in the area. Freelances don't want to waste time on stories they can't sell, so don't expect them to convey your press release to all the other media just to save you doing the work yourself.

You will never be able to find out how a freelance has treated a story because once the freelance has telephoned the copy it is up to the journalists in the receiving newsroom to decide how to write it up and treat it for presentation in a newspaper or broadcast. And it is the newspaper or broadcasting station that bears responsibility for the final product. This **lack of accountability** doesn't mean that the freelance journalists should be treated in any different way from other reporters; but it is worth remembering that you won't know what the freelance writes, and that his or her main interest is to fashion a story that will sell itself in competition with all the other bits and pieces of news on a news editor's desk.

Magazines, journals and the left press

Magazines

The British magazine industry is enormous. Some 4,500 titles are published each year, and hundreds more are being launched or folding in any twelve-month period.*

They range from the big women's weekly magazines with circulations of over a million, to obscure academic quarterlies. Magazines like *New Statesman, New Society, The Economist, Spare Rib*, are obvious targets for stories involving trade-union, minority group or community struggle. But even the more general magazines will publish hard-hitting material.

Woman's Own at one point published a feature on home-workers. The article centred on a woman who was sacked from her job sewing on tassles to Leeds United supporters' scarves. Her pay came to 17p an hour and the article described other

* In autumn 1979, a new magazine called *Now!* is being launched as a weekly news magazine aiming at being a British equivalent of *Time*.

PERTH (Tayside Region)

527 R W KEMP, WILLIAM, 49 Priory Place, Perth PH2 0EA. General news and sports reporting, features all subjects, with special emphasis and expertise on agriculture, horticulture, theatre, education, hotels, tourism. Tel: Perth (0738) 26795.

528 R MAULE, DAVID T (Press News Service), 15 Viewlands Place, Perth PH1 1BS. General news and sport coverage of Perth and the Tayside Region for press, television and radio; courts, crime, local government, soccer. Tel: Perth (0738) 23630 and 23980.

See also BOWATER, PETER & GEORGINA, ref 142; ELDER, IAN, ref 169; LITTLE, GEORGE, ref 136; SUTHERLAND, SANDY, ref 148.

PETERBOROUGH

528A R W B BEASLEY, PAT, 2 Kesteven Close, Market Deeping, Peterborough. General news, sport, newspaper design. Tel: Market Deeping (0778) 344481.

529 Pj P GARRATT, GEOFF, 48 High Street, Sawtry, Huntingdon, Cambs PE17 5SU. General news, features and sports coverage of East Anglia and the East Midlands. Tel: Ramsey (0487) 830297.

530 Pj P LOWNDES, GRAHAM (Mid Anglia Press & TV Services Ltd), 112 Broadway, Peterborough PE1 4DG, and 27A London Road, Peterborough PE2 8AN. Press photography, news and general. Television newsreel feature and documentary filming. Wire machine. Tel: Peterborough (0733) 65561 and 52731.

531 · R MUNNINGS, BILL, 7 Wyman Way, Orton Waterville, Peterborough PE2 0HA. General news, features. Tel: Peterborough (0733) 232883.

532 R W B NEEDLE PRESS SERVICES (Rex Needle), 31 Lincoln Road, Northborough, Peterborough PE6 9BL. General news, features, sport. Tel (24 hour service): Market Deeping (0778) 342550 (2 lines).

PETERSFIELD, Hants

533 R DIGBY, DOROTHY MAY (DOT), Inholms, Snailing Lane, Greatham, Liss, Hants GU33 6HQ. Local correspondent with extensive contacts and knowledge of people and organisations in Liss, Greatham, Hawkley and Selborne area. Tel: Blackmoor (042 07) 376.

See also WATTS, JOHN, ref 575.

PLYMOUTH, Devon

534 Pj BANKS, MIKE (Michael E.B. Banks), 131 Southland Park Road, Wembury, Plymouth, Devon PL9 0HH. Articles and pictures on defence, polar exploration, mountaineering, adventure pursuits, Liberal politics. Tel: Wembury (0752) 862241.

535 Pj P ROBERT CHAPMAN PHOTOGRAPHY (Robert Chapman). 54 North Hill, Plymouth, Devon PL4 8EU. General press photography and photojournalism, covering Devon and Cornwall. Tel: Plymouth (0752) 266919. Home: Ivybridge (075 54) 2656.

536 R W B ENDLE, RUFUS (Plymouth News Services Ltd), 171 Elburton Road, Plymouth, Devon PL9 8HY. News, sport, public relations. Coverage Plymouth and district. Tel: Plymouth (0752) 24548. Home: Plymouth (0752) 42232.

537 R W B GREENAWAY, JEREMY, 10 Holcombe Drive, Plymstock, Plymouth, Devon PL9 9JD. Radio and TV researcher/reporter. News scripts and features. Specialisation: marine and yachting. Tel: Plymouth (0752) 43230.

Page from the 1977 NUJ *Freelance Directory* listing freelance journalists.

home-workers in Leeds and elsewhere who were appallingly exploited. More important, the articles mentioned an organisation campaigning for home-workers, and as a result of the article many other home-workers had the confidence to come forward and join both the London Homeworkers Campaign and relevant unions.

Trade journals

Every industry, profession, craft or business has a trade magazine. The building industry has several, while the publishing industry is dominated by just one – *The Bookseller*.

Most of the trade press's revenue comes from firms whose activities are reported in the shape of advertisements about jobs, new products, company reports and special promotions.

The trade press tends to be oriented towards the management point of view. The pro-management line of some trade journals is clear from this internal document (issued in 1971) about the Thomson-owned *Construction News*:

> In order to sustain and develop the paper, recognition must be given to the importance of that part of the readership market which has executive authority or the readership market buying influence in the industry . . . The level and standard of reporting and general content of *Construction News* should reflect this recognition.

Most trade journals run on a shoe-string staff who welcome any professionally produced press release, speech or statement.

The socialist press

The left-wing press in Britain has more impact than the sum of its parts. Although it is divided up into small-circulation papers and magazines, it is followed closely by political and trade-union activists.

The Communist Party's *Morning Star*'s circulation is tiny (22,000) – but it is read by a large number of trade-union officials. The daily newspaper, *Newsline*, produced by the Workers' Revolutionary Party, sells fewer than 10,000 copies – but its pictures and news coverage of strikes boost morale on the picket lines even if its sectarian politics are ignored. *Socialist Worker* and *Socialist Challenge* have readerships far beyond their sponsoring organisations (Socialist Workers' Party and the International Marxist Group). *Socialist Worker*, in particular, has had a powerful agitational role amongst young workers in the 1970s. *Tribune* and *Labour Weekly* are **influential** because they get read by Labour MPs and councillors.

All the left-wing papers from their different political perspectives are at least united in being on the side of the workers. They act as an antidote to bias in the capitalist media. The wider the circulation and readership they have the better. **Workers and other activists should always send press releases or write their own stories for the left press.**

The left press publishes many stories which the mainstream media would not touch. Some of these stories will then be picked up by Fleet Street, which would otherwise have ignored them.

In 1976, the *Morning Star* published details of secret manoeuvres by Buckingham Palace to protect the confidentiality of the Queen's investments. The story was used on television and radio.

In 1977, *Socialist Challenge* revealed the contents of a speech made to a private meeting by Sir Richard Dobson, chairman of British Leyland. In it he referred derisively to 'wogs'. Fleet Street and American newspapers picked up the story and in the resulting furore Dobson had to resign.

After the 1978 TUC Congress, *Socialist Worker* ran a story about two-way mirrors installed in the foyer of the Brighton Conference Centre, which were used by the police to spy on delegates. The story was picked up by the *Sunday Times* and given national prominence.

As well as the papers connected to specific parties, there are other magazines that take up a radical position in their journalism – *The Leveller* and *Time Out* in London, *Rebecca* in South Wales.

Several towns and cities also have radical monthly or weekly newspapers: for example, *Broadside* in Birmingham, *York Free Press* in York, *Islington Gutter Press* in North London. The editors of all these papers welcome news and contributions.

Trade-union journals

Trade-union journals have improved immeasurably in recent years. More and more of them are being produced by teams of professional journalists with real commitment to their unions. There used to be endless pictures of General Secretaries doing the rounds. Now, there are more and more features about issues outside the immediate interests of the union – the struggle against racism, international issues, the extension of workers' rights, for example.

Given its combined monthly circulation of 8,000,000 the power of the trade-union press has not yet been properly utilised. However, trade-union journal editors have now formed themselves into a special section of the NUJ, and in 1978 the TUC instituted an annual competiton for the best trade-union newspaper.

Workers should encourage their union journals to be as lively and vigorous as possible. **Trade-union journals should be sent copies of any press release or statement sent to the media.** (There is a full list of trade-union journals on page 211.)

Student newspapers

Universities, polytechnics, colleges of education all produce newspapers and magazines run by student journalists.

There are two main advantages in getting in touch with student newspapers:

■ students can help in raising cash and providing support in various campaigns and struggles

■ their articles and photographs about community campaigns or trade-union work can be pinned up or shown to your colleagues, and can help boost morale.

Students in art departments can also help you with your own posters or leaflets. Some universities and polytechnics also have film and television schools. The students have to make films as part of their studies, and they often produce them to a high professional standard.

> Students at the Central London Polytechnic made a 30-minute film in 1977 on the effect of dust as an industrial hazard. It was a superb indictment of management and government complacency. Made with the help of trade unionists, it was available to be shown at meetings.

Remember to be careful of libel when talking to student journalists. A professional reporter is trained to filter out libel, but a student journalist may be ignorant of newspaper law (see page 176).

Community newspapers, parish magazines, etc.

Every month, hundreds of small newspapers, journals and magazines are published by different local organisations. Tenants' associations, the local church, community-relations councils, street committees and local pressure groups are all busy producing papers. These are all read eagerly by their target audiences.

There is a common assumption that the only media that count are the main newspapers, television and radio – **ALL the media should be used to get a message over.**

Ethnic-minority press

The foreign-language ethnic press in Britain is becoming increasingly important. Two daily newspapers are published in Urdu, as well as a series of weekly papers and magazines in Bengali, Gujarati, Hindi, Punjabi and even one monthly magazine published in Tamil. (A full list is given on page 210.)

In addition, there are English-language newspapers written for the West Indian communities and three Greek weekly newspapers produced for the large Greek-Cypriot community.

Much of the news in the Asian newspapers is a re-run of political problems from Pakistan, Bangladesh or India. But, **with the growing understanding amongst ethnic-minority communities of the need to stand up against racist harassment in Britain, the ethnic press is forced to take note of these developments.**

> The September 1978 issue of *Banglar Dak* carried a report from Bethnal Green and Stepney Trades Council on the insecurity and fear felt by the Bengali community in Tower Hamlets because of the racist attacks by white hooligans.

> In June 1979 the *Daily Jang* published a list of prisons which were being picketed because they held immigrants who were being unfairly detained.

BBC External Services and international media

The BBC broadcasts 24 hours a day in English and several foreign languages all over the world. The BBC World Service is fervently listened to by British expatriates and that could include senior management of an organisation with which you are in conflict in Britain.

London is an international media centre aud all major foreign newspapers and television companies have correspondents here. Again, the way they report issues back to their respective countries may have an impact on a parent multinational firm or on the U.K. government when it digests foreign press reports.

Clearly, securing coverage internationally is not top priority except in rare cases. But the BBC External Services Newsroom (Bush House, Aldwych, Strand, London WC2) should be sent press releases going out to other broadcast media and where it is appropriate it may be worth contacting foreign correspondents based in London.

Teletext

New developments in television technology have made it possible for ordinary domestic television sets to be adapted so that they can receive and transmit to the viewer individual 'pages' of text. A private person with a specially adapted set can call up a page of news, for example, or select the weather information or the latest sports results, whenever he or she wants.

The BBC and ITV run teletext operations called, respectively, *Ceefax* and *Oracle*. Each has a small team of journalists writing and up-dating pages of news and information.

More significant is the Post Office's version of teletext, called *Prestel*. This is open to any organisation, firm, pressure group or individual who pays the appropriate fee: the message, advertisement, piece of news or whatever, is then put on to the *Prestel* computer, from where it can be selected by the person at home. The Post Office says it will not have any editorial control: it will continue to act simply as a common carrier.

With micro-technological advances bringing the cost of teletext conversions within easy reach of most wage earners by the mid 1980s, the implications of what is effectively a new medium – a cross between broadcasting and the printed page – have not been thought through. For the price of hiring a *Prestel* page, trade unions and political organisations will be able to give detailed instructions or analysis direct to individual members in their homes. Large companies and corporations with more cash at their disposal will be able to put over their point of view even more extensively.

With the Post Office refusing to accept responsibility over what is available on *Prestel*, the labour and trade-union movement should be considering whether this new and potentially very influential medium should be allowed to be dominated by the highest bidders, or whether some social control should be exercised.

Ownership

Newspapers

Although there are a few family firms which still own provincial newspapers, the days of individual proprietors like Lord Northcliffe and Beaverbrook are over. With the exception of the *Guardian* and the *Daily Telegraph*, all national newspapers are owned by UK conglomerates or by foreign-based multinational companies.

■ **News International** owns the *Sun* and *News of the World* as well as a chain of evening and weekly newspapers (Berrows) in Worcestershire and Herefordshire. It is controlled by an Australian-based company, News Ltd, presided over by Rupert Murdoch, who also owns newspapers and television and radio stations in the United States. At one stage, News International also owned nearly 40 per cent of the shares in London Weekend Television, and for a time Murdoch was directly involved in managing the company.

The *Sun* and the *News of the World* appear to be the most rabid of the pro-Tory, union-bashing newspapers in Fleet Street. In 1977, News International profits were £18·1 million.

■ **Atlantic Richfield** is the United States' fifteenth largest industrial corporation, with an income in 1976 of £329 million. n 1977, it bought the *Observer* from the Astor family. Soon afterwards, Conor Cruise O'Brien was installed as editor-in-chief – without any consultation with the staff, despite an elaborate mechanism that had been set up for staff consultation when the editor, Donald Trelford, was appointed.

O'Brien, was formerly Minister of Posts and Telecommunications in Eire, and had been responsible for official news censorship

■ **The Thomson Organisation*** owns *The Times*, *Sunday Times* and a chain of important regional newspapers, including those produced in Aberdeen, Belfast, Blackburn, Burnley, Cardiff, Edinburgh, Hemel Hempstead, Newcastle and Reading.

Full control of the Thomson Organisation was switched to Canada after the death of Lord Thomson in 1977.

Oil and the travel business account for a larger share of Thomson profits than newspapers. In 1977, the British Thomson interests made a profit of £22·5 million, of which £9·5 million came from regional newspapers.

* At the time of going to press it was unclear what the future of *The Times* and *Sunday Times* would be.

■**Reed International** is the biggest UK-based multinational with newspaper interests. Through one subsidiary, Mirror Group Newspapers, it owns the *Daily Mirror*, *Sunday Mirror* and *Sunday People* and the *Daily Record* and *Sunday Mail* in Scotland, as well as a group of provincial newspapers in Devon.

Reed International also owns IPC (International Publishing Corporation), which publishes more than 200 magazines including *Woman*, *Woman's Own*, *Woman's Realm*, *New Musical Express* and a wide variety of comics and trade journals.

■**S. Pearson and Son** owns only one national newspaper, the *Financial Times*. But its provincial-newspaper subsidiary, Westminster Press, has the largest single share of the provincial morning, evening and weekly market, owning more than a hundred titles. It controls daily newspaper production in Barrow, Basildon, Bath, Bradford, Brighton, Darlington, Oxford, South Shields, Swindon and York. *The Economist* is another subsidiary.

S. Pearson also have extensive interests in book publishing, including Longman and Penguin Books.

S. Pearson donated £10,000 to Conservative funds in 1977, as well as £1,500 to British United Industrialists and £1,000 to Aims of Industry. Lord Gibson is chairman of S. Pearson, while the Duke of Atholl is chairman of Westminster Press. Another member of the aristocracy, the Honourable Michael Hare, is chairman of Pearson Longman. Westminster Press profits in 1977 were £6·2 million.

■**Associated Newspapers Group (ANG)** is the newspaper group based on the *Daily Mail*. It is presided over by Lord Rothermere, who now lives in the South of France. The group's provincial daily newspapers include those in Cheltenham, Derby, Exeter, Gloucester, Grimsby, Hull, Leicester, Plymouth, Swansea, Stoke and Torquay.

ANG has substantially diversified out of publishing into restaurants, oil and transport. Associated Newspaper profits in 1977 were £12 million.

■**Trafalgar House** is the latest Fleet Street proprietor. In 1977 it took over the *Daily Express*, *Sunday Express* and *Evening Standard*, and in 1978 it launched the *Daily Star*.

Trafalgar House has its roots in property, but in the 1970s it diversified into shipping (Cunard) and hotels (the Ritz).

In 1977, its turnover was £587 million, to which its newspapers contributed 4·1 per cent.

Trafalgar's managing director is Victor Matthews, at one

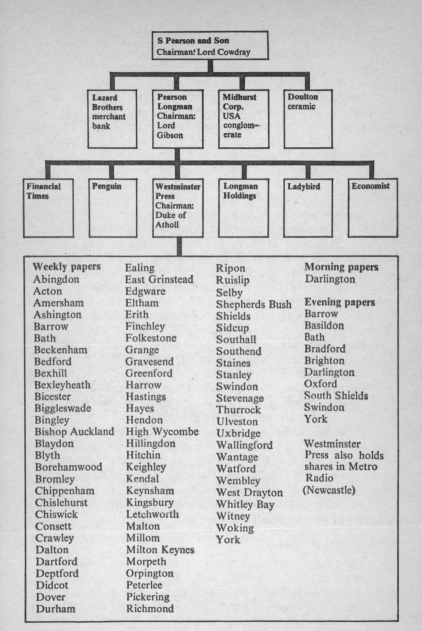

S Pearson and Son
Chairman: Lord Cowdray

| Lazard Brothers merchant bank | Pearson Longman Chairman: Lord Gibson | Midhurst Corp. USA conglomerate | Doulton ceramic |

| Financial Times | Penguin | Westminster Press Chairman: Duke of Atholl | Longman Holdings | Ladybird | Economist |

Weekly papers
Abingdon
Acton
Amersham
Ashington
Barrow
Bath
Beckenham
Bedford
Bexhill
Bexleyheath
Bicester
Biggleswade
Bingley
Bishop Auckland
Blaydon
Blyth
Borehamwood
Bromley
Chippenham
Chislehurst
Chiswick
Consett
Crawley
Dalton
Dartford
Deptford
Didcot
Dover
Durham

Ealing
East Grinstead
Edgware
Eltham
Erith
Finchley
Folkestone
Grange
Gravesend
Greenford
Harrow
Hastings
Hayes
Hendon
High Wycombe
Hillingdon
Hitchin
Keighley
Kendal
Keynsham
Kingsbury
Letchworth
Malton
Millom
Milton Keynes
Morpeth
Orpington
Peterlee
Pickering
Richmond

Ripon
Ruislip
Selby
Shepherds Bush
Shields
Sidcup
Southall
Southend
Staines
Stanley
Swindon
Stevenage
Thurrock
Ulveston
Uxbridge
Wallingford
Wantage
Watford
Wembley
West Drayton
Whitley Bay
Witney
Woking
York

Morning papers
Darlington

Evening papers
Barrow
Basildon
Bath
Bradford
Brighton
Darlington
Oxford
South Shields
Swindon
York

Westminster
Press also holds
shares in Metro
Radio
(Newcastle)

Lord Cowdray has now handed on control of his empire to a relative, Lord Gibson

stage a council member of the extreme right-wing Economic League. In 1977, Trafalgar House contributed £20,000 to Conservative Party funds.

■ **Other groups.** Of the national press, only the *Daily Telegraph* and the *Guardian* are owned by companies that rely chiefly on newspaper revenue for income. The *Daily Telegraph* is controlled by the **Hartwell family** with Lord Hartwell acting as editor-in-chief. The *Guardian* and *Manchester Evening News* are linked together in the **Scott family trust,** with the handsome profits of the latter helping to subsidise the former during the 1960s and early 1970s.

United Newspapers is another major provincial newspaper group, which controls morning and evening newspapers in Burnley, Blackpool, Doncaster, Leeds, Northampton, Preston and Wigan, as well as a chain of weeklies and the magazine *Punch.* United Newspapers has also made contributions to Conservative Party funds. Its chairman is Lord Barnetson, who trebles as chairman of Thames Television and chairman of the *Observer.* He was also chairman of Reuters between 1968 and 1979.

East Midlands Allied Press controls evening papers in Kettering and Peterborough as well as weeklies and magazines (1977 profits were £1·02 million).

Eastern County Newspapers enjoys a monopoly in East Anglia, with morning and evening papers in Norwich and Ipswich (1977 profits were £1·56 million).

Cities like Liverpool, Bristol and Nottingham have newspapers which are not linked with any other paper. But, in the West Midlands, the **Illiffe family** interests still control the *Birmingham Post* and *Mail,* the *Coventry Evening Telegraph,* the *Cambridge Evening News* and a chain of weeklies in the Black Country (they have also diversified into property, under the umbrella of **Birmingham Post and Mail Holdings Ltd**).

Television and radio

The BBC, of course, is not owned by anyone. It was set up as a private company in 1922, but it turned into a public corporation in 1927, just after its first Director-General, Lord Reith, had proved the fledgling corporation's worth to the state by refusing to broadcast the trade union's side during the General Strike. Such was the BBC's desire not to embarrass the government, that even the Archbishop of Canterbury was not allowed to broadcast a message of conciliation!

The BBC is controlled by a Board of Governors who are appointed by the Prime Minister. The Board of Governors in turn appoint the Director-General and other senior BBC staff.

The Home Office takes a close interest in BBC policy and, since the BBC is dependent on income from a licence fee the level of which is set by the government, there is close contact between senior BBC management and the senior civil service.

The 14 ITV companies (ITN is jointly owned by them) are separate companies. Thames Television is jointly owned by EMI and British Electrical Traction, while ATV Network is a subsidiary of the ATV Corporation presided over by Lord Grade.

Newspaper interests hold a large proportion of television company shares – in 1976, for example, Associated Newspapers had 37·5 per cent of the voting shares in Southern TV, while the Dundee-based publishing group D. C. Thomson had 24·8 per cent. The Thomson Organisation still has a quarter of both the voting and non-voting shares in Scottish Television.

As with ITV, commercial radio stations are separate limited companies. The legislation that set them up was intended to ensure that radio stations could not become part of other media conglomerates. However, because of a fear that local radio advertising would lessen the advertising income for the provincial and weekly press, the companies bidding for the radio franchises were obliged to make 10 per cent of the share capital available for local newspaper interests.

As well as more traditional investors, local cooperative societies and trade unions also invested in the new commercial radio stations. In Birmingham, a President of the Cooperative Party, John Parkinson, was appointed chairman of the Birmingham commercial station, BRMB. In Nottingham, a full-time official of the Union of Shop, Distributive and Allied Workers (USDAW), Syd Williams, was made a director of Radio Trent after USDAW had bought eight per cent of the shares.

Unions in the media

Newspapers

Ninety-five per cent of the journalists in Britain and Ireland belong to the National Union of Journalists, which was founded in 1907. The union has 30,000 members, of whom 9,000 work on provincial newspapers, 5,000 on national newspapers, 2,000 in television and radio, 5,000 in magazines; the rest are freelances, or work in public relations or for book publishers. There is also a small non-TUC organisation called the Institute of Journalists, which has 1,500 members, most of them senior executives or anti-trade-union refugees from the NUJ. The IOJ mainly operates as a strike-breaking task-force for newspaper employers.

Although journalists on Fleet Street and in national broadcasting are well paid (average salary of £8,000 in January 1979), their brothers and sisters in provincial newspapers are not so well off. In January 1979, the minimum rate for a qualified provincial journalist was still £70 a week. Provincial newspapers also have 2,000 apprentice journalists ('juniors', as they're called) employed on wages which are a proportion of the minimum rate. Juniors form the majority of the journalistic staff on weekly papers. Most are recruited locally by weekly paper editors and then go through a three-year training scheme. During that time they form a pool of cheap and eager labour.

The NUJ has become progressively more militant since the late 1960s. Starting with major Fleet Street strikes by individual chapels in defiance of the NUJ Executive, a general mood of wage militancy permeated the entire membership until the first-ever all-out provincial newspaper strike from 4 December 1978 until 22 January 1979 – which resulted in a trebling of the Newspaper Society's first offer.* (See Chapter 8 on making contact with NUJ chapels and branches.)

The print and mechanical unions in the newspaper industry have a craft history that in some cases goes back for more than a hundred years. The problems they have confronted in the 1970s are not all that new:

> In 1814, John Walter, the owner of *The Times*, successfully prosecuted twenty-nine compositors under the Combination Acts when they refused to handle the new printing machinery he wanted to introduce. In 1978, compositors on *The Times* – members of the National Graphical Association – found themselves facing the sack because they too were not prepared to work with new machinery unless it was introduced on satisfactory terms.

■ The **National Graphical Association (NGA)** is the union that organises compositors – the men (for there are very few women compositors in the industry) who take the journalists' copy and turn it into typeface suitable for printing.

* The Newspaper Society is the federation of provincial newspaper owners.

■ The **National Society of Operative Printers, Graphical and Media Personnel (NATSOPA)** organises both the people who look after the printing presses and the clerical and secretarial staff on a newspaper.

■ The **Society of Lithographic Artists, Designers, Engravers and Process Workers (SLADE)** organises the workers responsible for making pictures, blocks and plates.

■ The **Society of Graphical and Allied Trades (SOGAT)** is responsible for organising members in the distribution of newspapers.

Craft unions like EETPU and the AUEW also have a few members organised in chapels in some newspapers, while USDAW and the TGWU organise newspaper-distribution van drivers in some provincial cities.

Television and radio

Apart from the small craft unions (EETPU, NATKE), the main unions in broadcasting are:

■ the **Association of Cinematograph, Television and Allied Technicians (ACTT)**

■ the **Association of Broadcasting and Allied Staff (ABS)**. These two unions have voted in principle to merge to form:

■ the **Amalgamated Film and Broadcasting Union (AFBU)**.

The ACTT grew out of the British film industry and quickly established control of technical grades in commercial television after 1956. The ABS, which organises all grades in the BBC, was not registered with the TUC until 1963.

The ABS and ACTT share the organisation of technical and other staff in commercial radio. The NUJ organises journalists in the newsrooms in the BBC, ITV and commercial radio and was also organising national strikes in BBC and commercial radio in the 1970s. Some BBC Current Affairs producers, directors and researchers are in the ABS but, in commercial television ACTT has complete organisational control of producers and directors and shares with the NUJ the organisation of researchers. ACTT has a closed shop in ITV, whereas the ABS has failed to persuade the BBC to concede a closed shop. However, when it finally goes ahead, the merger of the two broadcasting unions will mean a much stronger trade-union involvement in the BBC. Broadcasting journalists in the NUJ have recognised the advantages of having a single union for broadcasting by agreeing joint working practices at national and local level with the other broadcasting unions.

4.

How news is made

What is news? / how is news made? / good news

What is news?

According to Harold Evans, editor of the *Sunday Times*:

News is people. It is people talking and people doing. Committees and Cabinets and courts are people; so are fires, accidents and planning decisions. They are only news because they involve and affect people. (*The Practice of Journalism*, Heinemann 1963)

There is another, more famous definition of news: 'Dog bites man is not news: man bites dog is.' It's a statement which sums up what journalists are looking for:
- conflict (man versus the dog)
- pain (it hurt the dog)
- unusual behaviour (have you ever heard of it happening?)
- emotion (man and dog must have been worked up).

This is what constitutes news, and it is what we enjoy reading or watching.

Lord Northcliffe, one of the original press lords, had a more shrewd definition: 'News is what somebody somewhere wants to suppress; all the rest is advertising.'

Journalists will look for the following points to see if something is newsworthy:
- conflict
- hardship and danger to the community
- unusualness (oddity, novelty)
- scandal
- individualism

It is far better to accept these 'news values', and try to relate them to a conscious decision to seek out and use the media, than to decide that it's not worth the effort just because a journalist does not automatically share your own idea of what is important and newsworthy.

How is news made?

Strikes, planning protests, sit-ins, elections, go-slows, deaths – all of these *happen* – but news is **made.** What you see on television or read in the papers is a **manufactured** product. There is a chain of production in the manufacture of news between the event taking place and the reader or viewer becoming aware of it through the media.

The raw material goes through various refining processes and **can be substantially altered** at each stage of the chain of production. There is a formal division of labour, with different journalists having precisely defined, distinct functions:

■**reporters** produce copy but do not usually see what happens to it once it is handed over, although this is less true on small weekly papers and magazines.

■**sub-editors** re-write the copy, shorten it, give it a new emphasis and do all this without having been to the scene of an event or having spoken to any of the participants.

Most journalists, when accused of distortions in a report, offer the excuse that changes were made after the copy was handed in – there is always someone else down the line to blame.

News also costs money. In 1978, it cost about £40,000 in salaries, expenses and overheads to keep the *Guardian*'s three industrial reporters in action.

This expenditure had to be justified in terms of news gathered and copy produced. News is always around – it has to be, otherwise newspapers would vary in length from day to day and *News At Ten*, for example, would not fill its uniform 30 minutes.

The process of producing a newspaper or news programme is much the same, whether you are a tiny weekly newspaper, a local radio station or a Fleet Street newspaper. Three over-lapping processes are involved:

■origination: where news comes from
■selection: which news is used
■treatment: headlines and layout.

Origination

The raw material for news can come from anywhere. Getting it has far more to do with routine work than with imagination. For example, a reporter in a provincial newspaper or radio newsroom does one particular chore two or three times a day – calling the information room of every police station in the coverage area. 'Anything happening?' asks the reporter, and the policeman passes on whatever has been reported to the control room from the policemen on the beat or in their cars. It is from that simple call that a host of stories – accidents, deaths, crimes of all sorts – comes each day. Similar calls are made to fire stations and ambulance headquarters.

Much less news is phoned in by the public than is generally thought to be the case. In any case, news from an unreliable source (and there is no way of checking who is talking at the other end of a telephone) must always be checked out with a source that can be confirmed – which in the case of an accident or crime will mean the police, or, in the case of a trade-union story (say, a sudden walk-out, which you decide to telephone to the local paper), the full-time official or, more probably, the company itself. **An unknown voice on the telephone will not automatically be believed and the information given will always be checked.**

On weekly papers, reporters will also regularly phone up people in news-making positions – councillors, town-hall officials, doctors, publicans, trade-union officials, branch secretaries – for a chat and to find out if anything unusual has happened.

By far the most important sources of news are **regular events** – court hearings, council meetings, other public-body hearings, VIP visits, trades-council meetings, political-party events, coroner's inquests, association dinners, and all the other scheduled happenings in the social, economic or political life of the community.

Each day, every newsroom will get letters, press releases, statements, which will be scanned for news. Newspapers (and television and radio stations) work far in advance of their formal publication dates or transmission times, and their most important tool in the business of news origination is the **news diary**, which lists day by day the events known to be taking place which might provide a news story.

Of course, not every event will produce a story. It is the job of the reporter to try and assess, either on the phone or by attending an event personally or going to see the appropriate person, the strength of a story – that is, whether or not it should be written up and included in the paper. Reporters therefore are significant originators of news.

Finally, one of the big sources of news origination is all the other newspapers, magazines, and television and radio programmes.

> One Monday morning while this author was working for the BBC, one of the journalists on the 6 p.m. news programme came into the morning conference, slapped a great pile of cuttings from the Sunday newspapers on the table and announced, 'I've had a lot of good ideas over the weekend.' The conference broke up in laughter as he was one of the most unimaginative journalists in the BBC – and what he really meant was, 'A lot of other journalists have had ideas which I've seen in articles or news stories. I think we could repeat them on television.'

The flow of news stories from organisation to organisation is partly hierarchial, partly circular. Regional evening papers cull a lot of stories from the more numerous weekly papers and, in turn, Fleet Street gets many of its stories from the evening papers. Television and radio are more directly involved in this parasitical process, since broadcasting news has developed no grass-roots news-gathering system. There are only 2,000 broadcasting journalists compared with 14,000 in newspapers.

Selection

The process of selecting which items will be turned into the stories you read or hear goes on all the time and is influenced by a number of factors.

The person in charge of news selection in most operations is called the **news editor**. It is he (or, very occasionally, she) who decides *what* stories will be covered, *which* stories will be given to *which* reporters or specialist correspondents, and *what angle* he is looking for. Sometimes he briefs the reporter down to the tiniest detail – whom to interview or phone up, what kinds of quotes are wanted and whose views should be ignored.

News editors work under great pressure. They have to make snap decisions and will always worry that they are committing a reporter to a story that will turn out to be no good. They have to rely to a certain extent on 'what worked before', which can lead to a stereotyped approach to news events.

In the bigger newsrooms (in evening papers, national newspapers and broadcasting), below the news editor is a journalist known as the **copytaster**. It is his or her job to have a quick look at all the stories from outside sources (stories from the Press Association and other news agencies and from freelances; press handouts and statements or stories handed in). He or she then

PA

1 List

DIARY AND SCHEDULE FOR FRIDAY, MARCH 9, 1979.

Industrial news continues to make the main running. We shall have
a story on the Health Service disputes and the return to work of
many ancillary staff. Nurses' leaders are seeing Health Secretary
David Ennals over their pay claim. Reaction is expected to the
announcement that miners' leader Joe Gormley wants to retire. The
Scottish Labour Party conference will have devolution on its mind,
and Mrs. Thatcher is visiting the West Country.

Foreign have a story on President Carter's
peace mission to the Middle East. The sports file will be dominated
by team news on tomorrow's heavy soccer programme, which includes
four FA Cup ties.

GENERAL NEWS DIARY:

1000 LONDON: Arab terror case continues, Old Bailey (staff)

1000 LONDON: Judgment of legality of Imperial Tobacco's
Spot the Ball competition, Appeal Court (Law Service)

1000 WINCHESTER: Trial continues of businessman accused of firing
rifle at police officer, Crown Court

1000 YORK: Hull prison officers' trial continues - Crown Court
(staff)

1000 PERTH: Scottish Labour Party conference opens at City Hall
(staff).

1015 SOUTHAMPTON: Transport Secretary William Rodgers tours
Southampton docks.

mf 0802 9/3 rf

nnn a 1 list

PA
2 List
General News Diary continued

1030 CORNWALL: Margaret Thatcher visits the west country. She
visits Launceston factory (1030). Camelford cattle market (noon).
Camelford trout farm (1510) Wadebridge Town Hall (19.30).

NOON CARDIFF: Scot Nat MP, George Reid, issues statement on talks
with Plaid Cymru (staff).

NOON LONDON: Building Societies Association meets to consider
mortgages. Park Street. (staff).

1230 CHESTEJFIELD: Funeral of Tom Swain MP at Chesterfield
Crematorium.

1300 YORK: Edward Heath speaks at Central Hall, York University.
He is going on to Bradford Univeksity (4pm).

1400 LONDON: Students march from Waterloo Station to Speakers'
Corner in grants protest (staff).

COMMONS: Private members' motions.

mf C805 9/3 rf
nnn a 2 List

PA

3 List

UNSCHEDULED

- BBC TV black-out threat over ''punch-up'' dispute

- Judgment expected in Lady Ann Tennant's copyright action (law
Courts).

- High Court proceedings expected in London over woman who
defied Burnley parks dogs ban.

- Mr. Justice Melford Stevenson hears rape case, Old Bailey

- New Rector of Edinburgh University - announcement this
afternoon.

- Health Service disputes.

- Possible further reaction to the Times peace formula.

- Back-bench attack on Pay Comparability Commission.

- Comment on Joe Gormley's planned retirement.

end 0815 9/3 rf
nnn a 3 List

A PA schedule.

has to decide whether to pass the story on for further consideration or to 'spike' it.* The copytaster's job is an important first stage in the selection of news. **If a story fails at that point it will effectively be lost as far as that paper is concerned.**

However, there are ways of getting straight to the news editor, bypassing the copytaster. One of the most obvious is for a reporter to arrive with a story he or she has obtained privately, either via personal contacts or because someone phoned him directly. Depending on his estimation of the reporter, the news editor may or may not decide to use the story. But he is quite likely to pay attention if it is a fellow professional who is telling him that something is newsworthy.

Ultimately the most important single arbiter of what goes into a paper or a television news bulletin is the **editor**. On big papers he will be far removed from the minute-by-minute decisions taken by the copytaster/news editor team, but in a weekly paper he (and again there are very few women editors in newspapers or women programme editors in radio and television) may be the person who makes the final decision on nearly all stories.

Even if the degree of direct supervision varies from organisation to organisation, the editor is central in laying down the overall news approach of the paper. The editor does this at a conference held each morning where all the department heads – news editor, features editor, woman's page editor, sports editor, etc. – attend and discuss the prospects for the day. Already the list of main events that day – the 'schedule' – will have been drawn up, and the editor will give direct instructions or strongly hint which stories he thinks are important and how they should be covered. Later in the day there will be another conference, when final decisions are taken on what the pattern of stories in the paper is to be. If an editor considers a news item important, it will be in the paper. **Getting the editor on your side is therefore the single most important step towards having your news and point of view selected for use.**

A big edition of a major daily or evening newspaper will contain 140,000 words – about twice the length of the average paperback novel. The search to fill those pages and find those

---

* 'Spiking' is a piece of journalistic jargon: all copy that is not going to be used is impaled on a metal spike set in a wooden base. This action gives dramatic emphasis to the journalistic notion of 'killing' a story that is not to be taken any further – once the piece of copy is 'spiked', it is 'dead'!

words is continuous and wide-ranging. Although the **news pages** will most concern you if you have daily news items to place, **don't forget the other sections of the newspaper**: the features page, the **diary** and the **women's page** all need a constant flow of ideas and stories too. The editors of these different sections select what they want to cover and, although they are subject to the editor's final approval, they have considerable autonomy in the selection process. There is no permanently unchanging reason why women's pages should, as in so many cases they do, concentrate on fashion, cookery and household hints. The problems of women at work, the fight for equal pay, etc., can make good feature material for a women's page. A profile of a women trade-union official on a women's programme on local radio can be made as interesting as an interview with an actress visiting the local repertory theatre.

The business of selection cannot begin, however, until the stories have been proposed to the department editors – and **very few suggestions for possible coverage get sent in.**

Treatment

The final and most important link in the chain of production is the treatment of the story to make it ready for printing or broadcasting. Theoretically, newspapers could dispense with reporters altogether and simply cull news from press handouts and news-agency material. But they would still have to give instructions to printers on what size type should be used, what kind of type face, the width of the type, the size and shape of headlines, and a design for each page so that the different stories, headlines and pictures all fit together. This process is called **sub-editing (subbing,** for short), and it is performed by a journalist called a **sub-editor,** or **sub.** (See Chapters 9 and 10 for specific job functions in television and radio.)

In charge of the sub-editors is a **chief sub.** It is his or her job to allocate the stories as they come in to different subs. He/she also takes charge of designing the main news pages of the newspaper. He/she also looks at the subbed versions just before they get sent away to be printed – **and can make amendments that will be unknown to the reporters and the subs.**

The sub's job is also to look at the news copy and make sure it is written in accurate, clear English and in a manner that will conform with the newspaper's style. Reporters often complain that their original copy is completely re-written by subs, and subs, in turn, take pride in their ability to improve the copy

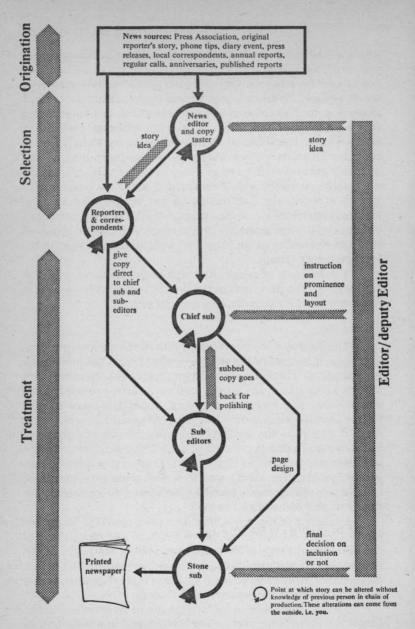

Origination

Selection

Treatment

Editor/deputy Editor

News sources: Press Association, original reporter's story, phone tips, diary event, press releases, local correspondents, annual reports, regular calls, anniversaries, published reports

News editor and copy taster

story idea

story idea

Reporters & corres- pondents

give copy direct to chief sub and sub- editors

instruction on prominence and layout

Chief sub

subbed copy goes

back for polishing

Sub editors

page design

Printed newspaper

Stone sub

final decision on inclusion or not

Point at which story can be altered without knowledge of previous person in chain of production. These alterations can come from the outside, i.e. you.

The news production line

submitted to them. Part of the subbing process is technical – checking for correct spelling of names and for accuracy of facts, figures and dates, and looking out for any potential legal problems like libel – but the sub also feels, correctly, that creative and imaginative skills can be used in subbing, and he or she enjoys deploying them. There is one big problem, however: **the sub has not been involved with the original source of the story.** The sub has not spoken to any of the participants or seen the situation described in the reporter's copy. He or she may, of course, be working from original source material, such as a government report, or council-committee minutes or a press handout. The sub's activity is none the less purely a literary one, concerned with *writing* and with **presenting** the news in a way that will guarantee the successful retailing of the commodity he or she is involved in producing.

In journalistic theory, the sub should check with the reporter before rewriting any story in such a way as to alter the sense, even in the most marginal way (as, for example, re-ordering lists of facts as they appear in the reporter's copy). **In practice, subs have to work very fast and in most cases, do not have time to check a proposed rewrite with the original reporter.**

One of the most important rewriting jobs that a sub undertakes is to cut copy. Sometimes this is done for the sake of the story, to make the meaning more clear; usually, though, it is simply done to shorten the number of column inches taken up by one story in order to release space for another.

In a telling example in his journalist's textbook on subbing, Harold Evans, editor of the *Sunday Times*, sets side by side a letter sent to him for publication and its subbed version, which conveys the same sense but uses only a third of the words. What is more, Evans's subbed version puts over the message with greater clarity and impact.

The original letter read:

We are all aware of the significant need to maintain uppermost in the mind of mankind the stark need of avoiding bloody international conflict. One method by which this can be nurtured is to revive the solemn aspect of the great loss of life which has resulted from such catastrophic struggles, within the theatres of war. The attachment is associated with such an endeavour . . . I would appreciate a directive to your staff to review the attachment for the purpose of orienting this information so as to evolve a

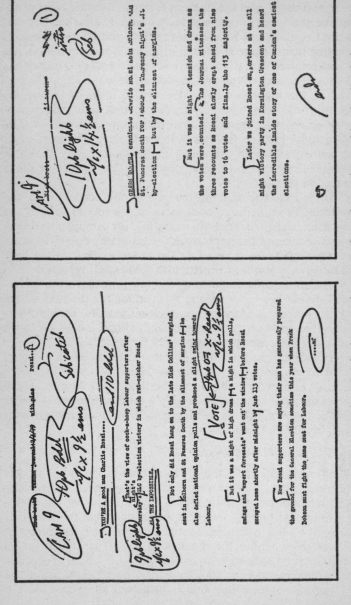

How the printed page is put together. Original type-written copy from the reporter, with sub-editor's instructions.

Conservative Central Office

NEWS SERVICE

Release time: Immediate/Embargo 9th March 1979

Comment by Geoffrey Finsberg M.P. (Camden, Hampstead), Vice-Chairman of the Conservative Party and the agent for the by-election in Holborn and St. Pancras South on Friday, 9th March 1979

"The result in Holborn and St. Pancras South is most satisfactory, bearing in mind the scurrilous campaign of the Labour Party. All credit is due to our candidate, Chris Radmore.

"What this result shows, is a test engagement with Labour, is the need for an early General Election. If this were repeated in a General Election it would give the Conservative Party over 15 more seats in Greater London.

END

Issued by Publicity Department, Conservative Central Office, 32 Smith Square, London SW1 01 222 9000

Can 9
72 pt 08
72 pt x 3

ROSSI = DOES IT!

(Can 9)
30 pt 04
18 pt x 5

leave reverse
indite ono of black

RAT-CATCHER GRABS ELECTION VICTORY FOR LABOUR

Press release converted into copy for the printer.

Headlines with picture captions.

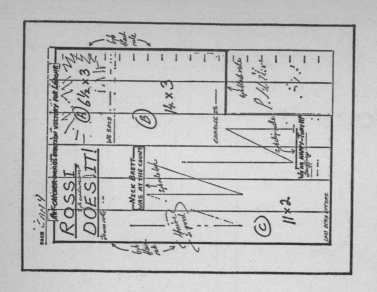

Page layout.

Rat-catcher grabs election victory for Labour

Rossi does it!

The people's choice

WE SAID it on the front page of The Journal, now the people have proved we were right.

GRASS ROOTS candidate Charlie Rossi held Holborn and St Pancras South for Labour in Thursday night's GLC by-elections — but by the slimmest of margins.

But it was a night of tension and drama as the votes were counted. The Journal witnessed the three recounts as Rossi slowly crept ahead from nine votes to 16 votes and finally the 113 vote majority.

Later we joined Rossi supporters at an all night victory party in Mornington Crescent and heard the incredible inside story of one of Camden's craziest elections.

Nick Brett was at the count

YOU'RE A GOOD man Charlie Rossi . . .

That's the view of cock-a-hoop Labour supporters after Thursday night's GLC by-election victory in which rat-catcher Rossi did THE IMPOSSIBLE.

Not only did Rossi hang on to the late Dick Collins' marginal seat in Holborn and St Pancras South by the slimmest of margins — he also defied national opinion polls and produced a slight swing towards Labour.

Vote

Now Rossi supporters are saying their man has generously prepared the ground for the General Election sometime this year when Frank Dobson must fight the seat for Labour.

But it was a night of high drama — a night in which polls, swings and "expert forecasts" went out the window — before Rossi scraped home shortly after midnight by just 113 votes.

According to one of our sources, only the night before (Wednesday) dejected Labour Party agent John Braggins was preparing Party workers for a 700 vote defeat.

At Tory headquarters in Argyle Square, agent Marion Wright was confidently talking about a 1,200 vote victory for Conservative's Chris Radmore as "reasonable" and a 600 vote margin as "unreasonable", according to another Journal source.

First signs of a Rossi victory came around 11 pm when the first count showed him just nine votes ahead of Radmore.

But it was an hour and a half and two recounts later before the Tories finally conceded defeat.

After a second recount at 11.20 pm put Rossi further ahead by 16 votes, the returning officer ordered a complete re-count.

When the bundles of votes were untied, it was discovered that one had been wrongly labelled for Radmore.

But even then — with Rossi now 113 votes ahead — Mrs Wright, after urgent, whispered conferences with Tory workers, argued unsuccessfully for a fourth recount.

She even went as far as checking every bundle herself with the help of the candidate before they finally admitted to defeat around 12.30 am.

Radmore, now a third time loser in Camden elections, was helped, visibly shaken, from the Town Hall by his wife. He declined to shake hands with the victorious Rossi.

But some local Tories did congratulate Rossi and it is now understood that the Conservatives feel their choice of Radmore — an outsider from Ealing — was the wrong one.

The Conservatives vice-chairwoman Lilian Davies told The Journal: "Personally, I feel our candidate was not quite the type for this area. He's a nice chap but I expect it's the end of him."

Radmore was still smarting this week from his defeat. He told The Journal: "I've got nothing to say to your paper — nothing at all."

In his victory speech Rossi said: "You're commonsense people in Camden and you won't be fooled by anyone."

In the only ugly scene of the evening, a small group of National Front supporters screamed hysterical abuse at Rossi.

Despite mass leafleting, loud hailer cars, and the help of Nazis from Islington, the Front failed miserably to whip up race hatred in Camden finishing well adrift of Liberal Tom Hibbert and only 172 votes ahead of the Independent Housewife candidate Helen Bunny.

At an all night victory party in The Mornington Arms, Labour supporters marvelled at the way Rossi - in a much reduced 31.8 per cent poll -- captured only nine votes less than Dick Collins in 1977.

With national opinion polls showing Labour trailing the Tories by 13 per cent, Rossi's amazing 0.11 per cent swing was attributed to his proven 25-year record of community service in Mornington Crescent.

"No-one, but no-one, except Charlie Rossi, could have pulled this one off," beamed one Labour worker.

Earlier Rossi while praising "the round the clock support" he'd received from Camden's Labour movement talked to The Journal about the split in the Party which at one time had threatened his campaign.

The split apparently centred around Elsie Cumley, the Regent's Park tenants' leader, who Rossi accused of smearing him because of his part in the recent NUPE strike for low pay

CHARLIE IS OUR DARLING! Victorious Rossi salutes his supporters with the help of wife Margaret (left) and campaign worker Noreen Tysoe. On the right is Labour Party agent John Braggins.

Mrs Cumley claimed she was too ill to do any campaigning this election.

But when pressed to say if she would have supported Rossi had she been well, she replied: "I'm not prepared to talk to you about it at all."

Jim Hewson, chairman of the Regents Park Labour Party and a caretaker on Mrs Cumley's estate, told us: "Elsie has a little bee in her bonnet about the NUPE strike and its effect on hospitals she's got it all wrong."

Rossi also slammed some of Labour's leading lights in St Pancras, whom he described as "dead from the ankles upwards"

In particular, he cited former St Pancras South chairwoman Gloria Lazenby; Labour activist Jack Firestein, and St Pancras North chairman David Webster as "notably absent" from the Rossi bandwagon

Secretary of St Pancras Labour Party, Gale Burns, who said he was too busy to work for Rossi admitted that the branch had organisational problems

"The branch has been virtually disbanded and we weren't in a position to get our election machinery grinding," he said "We did call on our members to vote Rossi "

The result of the GLC by-election in Holborn and St Pancras South was

Charlie Rossi (Lab)	5.946
Chris Radmore (Con)	5 833
Tom Hibbert (Lib)	437
Frank Theobald (NF)	372
Helen Bunney (Ind Housewife) . . .	200

● See letters page 18, and Jon Tulliver page 19

LAST DITCH EFFORT: Conservative candidate Chris Radmore and Tory agent Marion Wright deperately search for extra votes.

WE'RE HAPPY—TORY MP

GEOFFREY Finsberg, MP for Camden, Hamstead and vice-chairman of the Conservative Party said: "The result in Holborn and St Pancras South is most satisfactory, bearing in mind the scurrilous campaign of the Labour Party. All credit is due to our candidate, Chris Radmore.

"What this result shows, as a test engagement with Labour, is the need for an early General Election. If this were repeated in a General Election it would give the Conservative Party over 15 more seats in Greater London."

Printed page.

reasonably newsworthy article through your newspaper towards the end stated above.

Harold Evans's subbed version read:

Men need reminding of the horrors of war. One way to do it is to honour those who died and I would appreciate it if you could use the attached information for a report on our ideas.
(Harold Evans, *Editing and Design: Newsman's English*, London, Heinemann 1972.)

Much of the sub's cutting work does not rise to this lofty level of skilful précis. A lot of effort is poured into getting the first paragraph of the story – the 'intro' – right and the couple of paragraphs that follow on. On papers outside Fleet Street there is no time to polish up every single sentence in a typical story.
   The main danger lies in the sheer amount of straight-forward cutting that the sub has to do. In the hurry to get a story subbed, unless the story is so important that every tiny quote or fact is used, **crucial qualifying sentences or phrases can be lost.**
   The sub's excuse is that if the story is to be used at all, it has to be pared down. This is ten times more true of radio and television where, in terms of words used, news bulletins are much shorter. The total number of words used in the normal-length IRN bulletin is smaller than in a single column of the *Sun*.
   Finally, there is one more stage in the process when copy may suddenly be cut or altered even further – by someone called the **stone-sub.**
   The stone-sub works on the **stone** (newspaper-industry jargon for the workbench in the room where the page is finally physically put together) closely with the printers. The job can involve making last-minute cuts in stories for technical rather than editorial reasons, because of the need to fit columns of print onto a page. The **pressure to fit a story into a page design,** whether in the newsroom or at the last moment by the stone-sub, is the largest single factor behind quotes or counter-balancing facts being left out. Stone-subs do not have time to rewrite stories. It is usually a matter of ripping out a suitably sized paragraph to make the story fit on to the page.

Headlines

Books have been published devoted solely to the art of

headline writing. Well-written stories may sell newspapers, but it is the well-written headline that sells the story.

The most famous news editors in Fleet Street have made their names because of their original approach to layout, including the use of headlines. For popular papers like the *Daily Mirror* or the *Sun*, it is the **presentation** of news that sells the paper, as much as, if not more than, the news content itself. The best headline-and-layout subs in Fleet Street are very highly paid and are sometimes lured from one paper to another like top soccer stars.

The headline is controlled by the same values as news selection and treatment, only in a more distilled, extreme way. To persuade someone to read the story underneath (and possibly buy the newspaper if he or she is passing a news-stand), the headline has to be, in a literal sense, **sensational** – it has to create a sensation of interest and excitement, great enough to arouse a desire to read on.

Besides packing the necessary drama into the few words of a headline, the sub-editor will almost invariably reveal at the same time the **paper's attitude** to the particular story:

> A story in the *Daily Mail* about one NALGO member's opposition to the activities of a rank-and-file group inside NALGO was given the headline 'FIGHT TO SAVE NALGO FROM RED WRECKERS'. The alliterative 'red wreckers' is a perfect example of two words conveying drama, extremism and excitement. Only someone hardened to the *Mail*'s approach to trade-union news would have turned to the next page secure in the knowledge that the story was not going to live up to such a thrilling announcement.

The headline writer really comes into his own during a long-running dispute. With skilful use of headlines alone, she or he can help create a climate of hostility to strikers.

> Seven weeks into the 1977–78 firemen's strike, the *Daily Mail* front page (29 December 1977) was dominated by the headline 'IT'S TIME TO TALK AGAIN'. No named reporter was attributed to the story. The first paragraph read:
>
>> Firemen's leaders will face increasing pressure today from strikers to find a solution to the seven-week dispute.
>
> The implication of both headline and introduction are clear: the *Daily Mail* believes that the striking firemen and the employers/government should come to terms. It is straightforward anti-strike propaganda, but presented as news.
> The second paragraph went on to read:

A special *Daily Mail* survey of fire stations yesterday shows that strikers in many areas want the Fire Brigades' Union to call a special conference to consider the employers' latest offer.

The word 'survey' gives an authoritative ring to the story. But a careful reading of the full 707 words in it gives no indication of where the survey was carried out, who was interviewed, who did the interviewing or whether there was a shred of statistical reliability in the survey. In fact the two key questions that the *Daily Mail* claimed to have asked the firemen produced results that in no way justified the headline or first two paragraphs.

The questions and results were tucked away in the 15th paragraph of a 19-paragraph story, and were on Page 2, away from the dramatic headline of the front page:

If there was a ballot on the present offer how would you vote?

South	North	Total
yes	yes	yes
9%	6%	8·5%

Should the union conference be recalled?

South	North	Total
yes	yes	yes
47%	7%	32%

What the *Daily Mail* survey in fact showed was that fewer than one in ten firemen wanted to accept the proposed offer, despite the privations of a seven-week strike without strike pay and the miserable experience of picketing and poverty during the Christmas holiday.

A fairer and more accurate headline based on what the *Daily Mail* survey had established would have been, 'FIREMEN SAY FIGHT ON', or '90 PER CENT SAY NO TO 10 PER CENT!', and the intro, if it genuinely reflected the survey, should have read:

Britain's firemen are determined to hang on and bust the 10-per-cent guidelines, despite the worst Christmas many of them have ever experienced.

A special *Daily Mail* survey shows that fewer than one in ten firemen wants to accept the latest offer and although there is some support for re-calling the union's conference more than two-thirds of the firemen are determined to battle on.

This re-writing of the *Daily Mail* headline and intro is not some left-wing pro-union fantasy. It precisely corresponds to what the *Daily Mail* itself discovered and to what its statistical survey, printed towards the end of a long story, actually showed. The fact that the *Daily Mail* did print the result of its survey in the 15th paragraph on Page 2 is completely outweighed by the front-page impression created by the five-inch-high headline and strident first paragraphs. It is possible that the headline, appearing as it did on a day between Christmas and the New Year, when there wasn't much domestic news about and at a time of considerable concern about the development of the firemen's strike, helped to sell extra copies of the *Daily Mail* that morning. If so, the sub (although a front page like that would have involved a senior editorial executive decision) would have been well pleased with his or her journalistic salesmanship. Truth seemed to take second place.

Reporters will often dissociate themselves from headlines and the treatment of their stories. **It is an easy excuse. The division of journalistic labour in the production of news is precisely designed to remove direct individual responsibility for the end product.** It also helps to stop journalists, either individually or collectively, thinking constructively about control of the paper they work on. Although journalists have more rewarding and creative jobs than the average office worker, those working in mass-media production still see themselves as individual cogs in a machine. It is an enormous problem to persuade cogs that they can *control* the machine.

Deadlines

All the media are governed by deadlines. A newspaper's final deadline is not until the presses start rolling; for radio, it is when the newsreader opens his or her mouth. But all the media need to have their stories planned, to have begun subbing, to know where and when an event is happening, and to have planned the pages and schedules and programme running orders *well in advance* of the actual moment of the final deadline.

Deadlines will vary for different sections of a newspaper. The Atticus column of the *Sunday Times*, for example, has to be written, subbed and laid out by Friday, two days before publication date. The majority of interviews you hear on the Radio 4 *Today* programme will have been recorded on the previous day. On weekly newspapers the letters column and inside news pages will have been 'put to bed' (made finally ready for printing) on Monday or Tuesday, even though the paper isn't printed until Wednesday night. News magazines have a similar schedule to that of the weekly newspapers. The *New Statesman* has its main editorial conference on the Friday of the week before publication, while most of *Socialist Challenge* is designed and laid out on the Sunday before Wednesday printing day. The Sunday colour supplements are printed weeks in advance of their formal publication date, and the minimum deadline for anything in a Sunday colour magazine is at least six weeks before publication.

Deadlines in broadcasting can often be the most confusing element in understanding how television and radio work. These two are the most immediate media, but television in particular needs more advance notice than any other medium because of the logistical problems involved in getting cameras on the spot and getting the film processed. By mid-morning, most of the stories that will appear in the same day's *News at Ten* have already been decided upon and reporters and crews sent out. **Anyone wanting proper coverage on television should ignore the transmission time and realise that the effective deadline is several hours earlier.**

Newspapers, magazines and television programmes also like to keep a stock of undated features or films. These will be articles or filmed reports which do not have to be printed or shown very close to the time they are written or made. This is yet another factor which can work to the disadvantage of the people actually *involved* in the stories.

Women workers at the Fakenham shoe factory, which was taken over and run as a co-operative, badly needed publicity to sell the products being made by the work-in. They willingly allowed *Nationwide* to make a film. Six weeks later the work-in was nearly over but the film had not been transmitted. Eventually it did go out, but so late that it was of very little direct benefit to the workers.

Below is a guide to the working deadlines of most of the media, excluding the very big story which can always be accommodated at the very last moment.

■ **weekly newspapers:** 2–3 days before date of publication (e.g., Monday for a paper bought on Friday)

■ **morning newspapers:** up to 9.00 p.m., but morning newspaper coverage is planned by mid-afternoon the day before

■ **evening newspapers:** 11.00 a.m. for the same day

■ **local radio:** straight news, an hour before news bulletin time; interviews, at least three hours in advance

■ **regional television:** 11.00 a.m. of the day on which the programme is broadcast

■ **national television:** same except for lunchtime news

bulletins, where editors need to be told the day before if they are to organise coverage

■ **weekly magazines:** *at least* 3–4 days before publication, since most weekly magazines plan their contents at least a week ahead

■ **monthly magazines, including most trade-union journals:** two weeks ahead of publication date.

Good news

Not all news is pitched at the level of conflict, stress, trouble and strife. The basic service of the local weekly paper – 'hatches, matches and dispatches' (i.e., births, marriages and deaths) – is as humdrum as can be. Look through a weekly paper or a regional evening paper. There will be a story and picture about a new managing director of a local firm, about a police officer receiving a bravery medal, about a local soldier serving overseas, about a schoolgirl who has got to Oxford – the small change in the comings and goings of the community.

Those stories are not there by accident nor have they been dug up by reporters. The firm's PRO has sent in a picture of the new managing director and some biographical details. The police press office has provided the picture of the sergeant being decorated and sent him along to the newspaper office for the interview. The private sent out to Belize has been asked where his home town is and the army's well-staffed PR machine has got a picture and story into the local paper knowing very well that it will boost recruitment. The headmistress, delighted at getting a girl into Oxford, has rung up the news editor.

Trade unions and workers should make their news available to the local media in much the same way.

Here are ten commonplace events in a trade-union year which involve or have an effect upon the *people* in the community.

■ **The award of a long-service medal or celebration of somebody's 50 years as a union member.** There are always some nice memories of the 'things aren't what they used to be' variety locked away in the minds of older workers. Perhaps a worker has a photograph of himself in some trade-union situation 30 or 40 years ago. Dig it out and give it to the local paper. What changes has he seen? If he is a breezy personality, contact the local radio station.

■ **Local woman elected as TUC delegate.** The TUC is a major national event watched by millions on television. If a colleague is elected as a delegate, get some good quotes from her about what she expects from her time there, who she's eager to hear speak, how she feels about meeting well-known trade-union leaders, her ambition to speak herself, and what her husband thinks about being left at home while she has the week off in Blackpool or Brighton.

■ **Elections and appointments.** A new chairperson for the branch or district council is chosen. Put out a press release to the local papers, giving details of age, family, personal interests, etc., and some quotes about what he/she thinks of the new post. Where possible, send a photograph as well. This should be of as high a professional standard as possible (see Chapter 6).

If the appointment is that of a regional official, the union's head office should arrange for biographical details and pictures to go out to all media in the area. Even if the story doesn't get published in many papers it is a worthwhile exercise, since the picture will be filed for when the official is next in the news. It also means that the industrial correspondents, news editors and newsrooms generally can get a better idea of the face and person-ality of a new trade-union official. **Always include contact phone-numbers** at the foot of press releases announcing new elections or appointments.

■ **Charity fund-raising.** Many trade-union groups go in for some kind of charity fund-raising during the year. It can be for a local, national or trade-union charity. One of the most common is a sponsored walk.

> In 1977, Kentish Town members of the Fire Brigades Union roller-skated from London to Edinburgh. Dressed up in their uniforms, they made an excellent picture for their local weekly paper and gained a lot of useful sympathy a few weeks before the outbreak of their national strike.

A darts match or simply a social occasion may be used to raise funds for charity. If so tell the local paper. A press officer can write the report and send it in.

During a dispute, why not arrange an event to raise funds for local charity and involve striking and laid-off workers? A story beginning, 'Strikers forgot the bitter dispute for a few hours today when they staged a sponsored walk through the town centre to raise money for local children's homes' should help shift public opinion and sympathy.

■ **Visit of a national celebrity.** Never let a visit to your branch by a well-known trade-union leader go by without telling the local media. It may be that what he or she has to say is confidential to the meeting, but he/she can at least be photographed with local union leaders before or after the meeting. Liaise with his/her office and arrange a time when he or she will be free to meet the local journalists.

If the meeting is not private but no reporter turns up to cover it, make a careful note of what the visitor says and then send out a press release (see Chapter 5).

■ **Trade-union scholarships.** Educational achievement is a favourite subject for the media, especially for local weekly papers. A worker who wins a place at Ruskin or who gets a trade-union scholarship should always be interviewed for a press release, but remember to put the person's contact telephone-number at the bottom so that journalists can get their own quotes if they feel like it.

There are also dozens of trade-union residential courses for workers. Give details of local workers who win places on these, but it may be more interesting in these cases to wait until the course is over and *then* put out a press release. This should be in the shape of an interview, with the workers describing the course, how they enjoyed it, what they felt about the fact that although it was a trade-union course for working people it was held in a country mansion in rolling countryside.

■ **Branch anniversary.** Many of the older trade-union branches now have histories going back 50 to 100 years. If your branch or trade-union institution celebrates an anniversary (25, 40, 50, 60, 75 years), why not have a little party to mark the occasion and invite the local media? Dig out some old minute-books or posters, and write down the landmarks in the branch history (a famous dispute, a former member who has gone on to greater things, boosts in membership, etc.), add a few quotes of your own about the local union never being stronger and looking forward to another 25, 50 or 100 years' activity, and send it out as a press release.

Newsrooms like anniversaries. Twenty years in office, 12 months since the end of a bitter dispute – if a 'peg' like this can be provided there is more chance of coverage.

■ **A year of achievement.** This can be a variety of different things. You may be looking back on a year in which there were no industrial accidents in a factory because of a newly instituted trade-union safety committee; or on twelve months without strikes, with new production records set and with a massive increase in membership; or on a year in which workers' wages fell to an all-time low expressed as a percentage of the company's profits (worth looking out for when the company publishes its annual figures). Whatever it is, at least **let the local media know.**

■ **Christmas party for children.** Many trade-union groups hold a party at Christmas time for members' children. They are always jolly occasions and local newspapers like stories and pictures with children in them. Tell the paper when and where you are having the party and suggest they send along a photographer. Better still, persuade a leading local trade-union personality to dress up as Santa Claus and hand out the presents. If he is well-known as a militant, so much the better – the idea of a 'Santa strike-leader' would make any picture editor happy!

■ **100th/500th/1,000th/10,000th new member.** Whenever your branch or area or region signs on a new member who takes the total local membership over a particular level, there is some news 'capital' to be made. You can do this with a big fanfare, by arranging a ceremony and persuading a national leader to come and hand over the membership card, or more quietly by putting out a press release with some quotes from the local branch secretary and from the new recruit telling why he or she has joined. It is a useful way of emphasising the steady growth of trade unions, and serves as a reminder that unions are not just about General Secretaries appearing on television but are to do with ordinary people living next door.

5.

Press releases

Why we use press releases / how to write a
press release / points of style / using quotes /
speeches / the embargo / what a press release
should look like / different types of press
release / examples

Why use press releases?

The press release is probably the single most important
means of communication with the media initiated from the outside. Every day, busy regional newsrooms receive dozens of
press releases. Some are slick and expensively packaged – usually
when the news in them is of only marginal interest. Others are
illegibly scrawled in hand. A press release is a partially digested
helping of news, which can easily be made into the real thing by
the professional journalists in a newsroom. News editors and
journalists like press releases: they save work. The reporter or
sub values having the facts displayed in an accessible form, with
pointers for further information.

Producing press releases requires work and care. A typewriter is essential. A method of copying – duplicator or photo-
stat machine – is also necessary. A hand-written press release
won't be ignored, and if the story in it is important it will be
used; **but there is a hundred times more chance of having the
material used if it comes over as easy to read and,** from the technical point of view of the sub-editor and printer, **easy to handle.**

Many trade union and political-party offices have type-
writers and a duplicator. The ACAS Code of Practice on time off
for union representatives requires management to provide
facilities so that union representatives can carry out their duties.
These include access to a telephone, a notice board and a meeting
room. Where the volume of work justifies it, office facilities (such
as typing and duplicating) must also be provided.

Press releases have different functions. They:
- give advance notice of an event
- provide a report of a meeting
- convey decisions taken by workers
- announce new campaigns and provide progress reports
- give general background information
- give details of a report
- circulate speeches in advance

Press releases give their senders the chance to offer *their* selection of facts and views **without these being filtered through anyone else.** Furthermore, *you* can decide **when** to provide the information. You can also provide the information **in a more permanent form** than through an interview.

The benefits a press release offer you are that:
- you can think carefully before committing yourself to words
- you have a permanent record of what you say
- you have a better chance of arguing a case, or making a point, than you do in the atmosphere of an interview.

The benefits to the media are that:
- it is easier to read than their disjointed notes
- it can be kept for several days and not get mislaid
- it summarises the information and views you want to communicate to them.

How to write a press release

Basic rules

A press release is in all its forms essentially a news story. Whether a two-line announcement about a new appointment or a 10-page account of a complicated report, the press release has to obey the basic rules of news writing. The first rule learnt by every trainee journalist is to concentrate on 'the five Ws':
- **What**
- **Who**
- **Where**
- **When**
- **Why**

Every press release should begin with the four Ws, and you should start off by writing:
- **What** is happening
- **Who** is doing it

■ **Where** is it happening
■ **When** is it happening

What, Who, Where, When do not have to be in that order, but they should always be in the first sentence or two of your press release.

Here are some example first sentences of imaginary press releases to show how the four Ws are worked in automatically:

Workers	**Who**
at Blacking Ltd	**Where**
have said they will ban all overtime	**What**
starting next Monday	**When**

Members of Bolton's Women's Liberation movement	**Who**
will occupy	**What**
the city council chamber	**Where**
tomorrow (THURSDAY) afternoon	**When**

Shop stewards	**Who**
at one of Newcastle's biggest building sites	**Where**
have published	**When**
a list of one hundred major safety hazards on the site	**What**

The General Engineers Union	**Who**
has appointed a new regional officer, Mr John Black,	**What**
who will start work next month	**When**
to be responsible for GEU members in East Anglia	**Where**

The fifth W is **Why** something is happening. It is necessary to explain the reasons behind, or causes of, the situation that justify producing the press release. In practice it is simple. Take the last four stories. The second sentence answering the question **Why** follows naturally in each case:

Workers at Blackings Ltd have said they will ban all overtime starting next Monday. *Their action follows the company's refusal to start talks on a new grading structure.*

Members of Bolton Women's Liberation movement will occupy the city council chamber tomorrow (THURSDAY) afternoon, *in protest at the council's decision to close down a hostel for battered wives.*

Shop stewards at one of Newcastle's biggest building sites have published a list of one hundred major safety hazards on the site. *They are increasingly worried about the lack of safety precautions which could lead to death or serious injury.*

The General Engineers Union has appointed a new regional organiser, Mr John Black, who will start next month to be responsible for GEU members in East Anglia. *The appointment reflects the growth of the GEU in the region.*

The intro

The first sentence or two – in journalists' jargon, the 'intro' – can be the key to the success or failure of the press release. At the start of a day's work, a busy news editor will have a pile of press releases, statements and letters from which to select the items which will be turned into news stories by reporters or sub-editors. **There is rarely time to read through the full length of a press release,** so only the first few sentences are quickly scanned. The press release **has to catch the news editor's attention immediately** – to do that, the intro **has to contain the most interesting fact** about the issue or event.

It is easy for someone who is not a journalist to leave out the most important point in a story:

In February 1979, the editor of the *Landworker* (the journal of the NUAAW, the farm-workers union) received a story from a union member about an active member who had died. The story painted a wonderfully warm picture of the dead man's life and contribution to the union. There was one problem however – nowhere in the story was the dead man's name given!

The rest

Once you have got *who, what, where, when and why* out of the way in a simple, direct form, you can get on with the rest of the press release.

Essentially, a story is being told – much as you would give a factual report to a meeting.

Concentrate on facts. Give the number of people involved, the venue of a meeting; spell out first names, quote statistics (not 'the company made huge profits last year', but 'the company's profits were up by 46% on the previous year'). The same disciplines of factual reporting should be exercised throughout the press release. Put the facts into the press release in **descending order of importance.** The five Ws do not belong only to the first two sentences. Spell out the reasons *why* it is happening, *what* past or future action is involved, *who* else will be effected, *what* you hope to achieve and *what* other likely results will follow.

The headline

Choose a **simple** headline for the press release (usually a short version of the first sentence will do). Leave it to sub-editors to think up fancy headlines; yours is there to help the news editor spot the interest of the story.

Put a verb in it:

- SHOP STEWARDS VOTE FOR OVER-TIME BAN
- ANTI-FASCIST PICKET TO BE HELD OUTSIDE COURT
- PARENTS LAUNCH CAMPAIGN FOR NEW NURSERY
- MASS PICKET PLANNED FOR PRIME MINISTER'S VISIT

Points of style

Press releases are not essays in English literature, nor are they marked by journalists as if they were exam answers. Information and views should be presented, in a **clear, digestible form.** If you read newspapers and analyse the news stories you will find out that certain rules are in operation. These will vary between the quality and popular papers; but for the kind of press release intended for the majority of the media – the regional evening papers, weekly papers, local radio and local freelance agencies – the **terse, economical style** of the news stories in the *Daily Mirror* is worth aiming at.

Keep sentences short. A maximum of 25 or 30 words will do. That is not many words at all. The last sentence of the last paragraph, for example, has 50 words. That is acceptable in a book but looks stodgy in a press release. Another test is to **make sure that a sentence carries only one idea.**

Use the active voice:

don't write: 'A new campaign to get industry into the area was announced by trades council secretary, John Smith . . .'
but do write: 'Trades-council secretary, John Smith, announced a new campaign to get industry into the area . . .'.
don't write: 'A meeting will be held next Monday by workers . .'
but do write: 'Workers will meet next Monday . . .'

Do not express yourself negatively.

—don't write: 'GEU members have decided not to accept management proposals . . .'
but do write: 'GEU members have rejected management proposals . . .'.

don't write: 'Liverpool dockers have said they will not handle
goods bound for Chile . . .'
but do write: 'Liverpool dockers have said they will boycott
goods bound for Chile . . .'.

Use vigorous, even aggressive language. The journalists will
scan the press release for one or more of those accepted 'news'
points – conflict, unusualness, scandal, individualism. Help them
by constructing sentences which suggest action. Use verbs like:

- accuse
- act
- blame
- challenge
- confront
- demand
- deny
- fight
- refuse
- reject
- shock
- warn

Avoiding jargon

Trade-union language can be long-winded and evasive and
is often strewn with clichés and jargon. Here is a sentence from
the 1976 TUC Congress Report:

> It is because the EETPU takes the view that there is a
> distinct possibility of the discussions that have taken place,
> solidifying into legislative fact, and also, the considerations
> given to those discussions by the General Council, have
> been more in the abstract than in the real, my executive
> council considered it necessary to express in the terms of
> the amended motion a definition into a correct perspective
> of the debates and decisions of Congress on industrial
> democracy.

In a press release that sentence would kill any potential
interest in a newsroom. What the speaker means is:

> Legislation on industrial democracy is likely soon. The
> General Council's approach has been vague so the EETPU
> decided to table a motion making clear where Congress
> stood on the subject.

In formal motions and reports and statements following negotiations, trade-union language is sometimes deliberately opaque. It is trying to satisfy, simultaneously, the rank-and-file workers, the trade-union head office, the executive councils, the politicians and all the different elements in the employing company/ies – management, board of directors, shareholders. A press release has to be sharper, which means that **you have to select your target audience.**

While a lot of trade-union jargon is understood by workers and other trade unionists, it might as well be Martian for the majority of newspaper readers or *Nationwide* viewers. **Avoid abbreviations or short-forms,** such as 'Confed', when you mean the Confederation of Shipbuilding and Engineering Unions. (And go further to explain – in brackets – that the Confederation of Shipbuilding and Engineering Unions is the joint body for all unions in the local engineering industries.) You do not want to tell an experienced industrial correspondent the difference between a convenor and a district secretary, but it may be worth spelling out to a weekly newspaper that one is a kind of chairman of shop stewards, who remains a company employee and stays close to the work-force, while the other is a full-time trade-union official, responsible to the District Committee and ultimately to the general secretary and the national executive of the union for his decisions.

Most active trade unionists understand at once what the term 'status quo' means, and the implication of a 'return to the status quo' or the 'honouring of the status quo'. But there are many other people who *don't*. Therefore:

—don't write: 'The company is refusing to return to the status quo as per the national agreement . . .'
but do write something like: 'The company is breaking a national agreement by insisting on the introduction of new methods (or sacking of a worker) without going through discussions first . . .'.

Give a newsroom the benefit of the doubt about technical terms and internal union titles. You may feel silly writing out in full what is obvious to you but it can save the sub-editor confusion and mistakes.

The temptation to use jargon and short-forms is understandable. Some of the clichés of worker/employer relationships ('the offer is totally unacceptable', 'nineteenth-century conditions' 'attitudes that come from the stone age') are good fun, but remember that an idea or point expressed in a cliché devalues the thought behind it and lessens its impact.

One of the worst sins of trade-union language is unnecessary padding and the use of clusters of words as conjunctions or prepositions.

Avoid:

■ 'with regard to'
■ 'in connection with'
■ 'as far as that position is concerned'.

Rephrase:

■ 'in spite of the fact that' as 'although'
■ 'on account of the fact that' as 'because'.

Watch out for abstractions. If when you write, 'facilities on the site are minimal to non-existent' you mean 'workers have to urinate against a wall', then *say so*!

Avoid the use of 'situation'. 'The unemployment situation is getting worse' means 'More workers are on the dole'; while 'we could be facing a strike situation' means 'there may be a strike.'

Try and be clear and to the point and, whenever you write a sentence, examine it to see if some of the words are superfluous – you can nearly always find them in a first draft. **Cut them out** and you will be getting a lot closer to the sub-editor's heart and consequently to getting your facts and views marshalled as you want them into the newspaper.

In 1977, the TUC gave oral evidence to a committee chaired by Sir Harold Wilson, which was looking at the City. A senior TUC official produced the following sentence.

> I do not think we can say it is a black-and-white situation but in the 1980s what we are emphasising is that we are in a whole new ball game when we hope we will have a growth scenario when we believe that profitability in a secular as well as a cyclical sense will be important.

Although he would never have written down anything as nonsensical as this, it stands as a wonderful example of clichés, jargon, circumlocution all jumbled together and utterly mean-ingless at the same time. **Avoid this style at all costs!**

Using quotes

News is about people – people talking, being directly quoted; people describing what they have seen, what they feel and what they think. **Every press release should include direct quotation,** even at the most banal level ('I am delighted at being elected convenor. My first job will be to go for a big wage increase for my members.')

Sub-editors like quotes. They make a story come alive by personalising a narrative.

Quotes can also be used to get over strong opinions that would look out of place in straight narrative. For example, if local workers are angry about a visit by a government minister which has meant a lot of expensive preparation, you cannot expect a newspaper to print a press release which goes: 'hospital workers are to protest at the absurdly expensive visit of the Industry Secretary to the town's hospital next week.' As it stands, the sentence is far too opinionated. Place the reference to absurd expense in quotes, and all is well:

> Hospital workers are to protest when the Industry Secretary visits the town's hospital next week. 'It is an absurdly expensive day-trip', said union leader Tom Brown. 'The money should be spent on improving facilities for patients and staff.'

It is better to keep to unvarnished fact in the narrative part of the press release and use the quotes to add some personal life and opinion to the story. Even in the shortest press release you should include a couple of quotes. Aim to get a direct quote in within the first three or four sentences. So, taking one of our dummy press releases which showed how to work in WHO, WHAT, WHEN, WHERE, and WHY, let us insert a quote:

> Shop stewards at one of Newcastle's biggest building sites have published a list of one hundred major safety hazards on the site.
>
> They are increasingly worried about the lack of safety precautions which could lead to death or serious injury.
>
> 'No-mans land in World War I was a safer place than parts of the site when the weather is bad,' said Fred Green, chairman of the joint shop-stewards committee.
>
> 'This has to be the most dangerous building site in Britain. We want action to improve safety otherwise there will be a worker killed or badly hurt.'

From then on you can mix up narrative and quotes, one following logically from the other in the press release. So, continuing with that fictional press release:

Nearly half the hazards listed by the men are to do with poor scaffolding on the top half of the building. They are also very concerned about the lack of protection around the lifts and hoists used to take men and material to the upper storeys.

'Safety is bottom of the list of priorities for this company. I would like to see the chairman send his wife and family up and down that rickety old lift,' said Mr Green.

One serious accident was avoided narrowly last month when men noticed that a shaft through the centre of the building had been lined with inadequate materials.

The men are sending the list of hazards to local MPs and the Health and Safety Inspector in Newcastle.

'Now that the list has been made public we hope the company will act. If they do not, the only alternative will be industrial action of one sort or another to force an improvement in safety measures.

'We do not want a strike but if the company do nothing they will have one on their hands,' said Mr Green.

When writing out quotes, just **copy the style of punctuation from a newspaper story.** Break the quotes into paragraphs of three or four lines. Put inverted commas at the beginning of the quote and, if the quote goes on for more than one paragraph, at the beginning of each new paragraph. Then, to show the quote is over, put inverted commas at the end of it.

Identify the speaker in full after the first sentence or two, by adding: '. . . said Mr Fred Green, Chairman of the joint shop-stewards committee.' Thereafter, you can run on the quotes in consecutive paragraphs and simply put 'he said' at the end of the quoted direct speech. But if you intermix narrative and quotes, you should identify who is speaking by writing 'said Mr Green' at the end of each fresh introduction of a quote.

Try not to use indirect reported speech. If written as indirect speech, the last sentence of the press release above would read: 'Mr Green said that the men did not want a strike but if the company did nothing they might find one on their hands.' This does not have the same impact as a direct quote from Mr Green.

Sometimes journalists will turn direct quotes into indirect speech in order to make all the points flow together neatly in the structure of the story they are writing. It is better, however, to let the journalist decide what will be indirect speech by providing him or her with direct-speech quotes.

press release

NATIONAL UNION OF AGRICULTURAL AND ALLIED WORKERS

Issued by the Land Worker Publishing Co. Ltd.
Headland House 308 Gray's Inn Road London WC1
Telephone: 01-278-7801

PRESS INFORMATION

7th November, 1978.

MASS LOBBY AT FARMWORKERS' PAY NEGOTIATIONS

Negotiations over farmworkers' pay were deadlocked after
the 3rd November meeting of the Agricultural Wages Board.

The Workers' Side of the Board is asking for £80 for a
35 hour week. The farmers are sticking to a very narrow
interpretation of the 5 per cent pay guidelines which would
add much less than 5 per cent to the basic minimum wage.

SO WHEN THE BOARD MEETS NEXT - ON THURSDAY, DECEMBER 7TH -
THE NUAAW IS ORGANISING A MASS LOBBY. THIS WILL TAKE PLACE
AT 12 NOON OUTSIDE THE MINISTRY OF AGRICULTURE IN WHITEHALL
PLACE, AND WILL BE ADDRESSED BY GENERAL SECRETARY, JACK BODDY
WHEN THE AGRICULTURAL WAGES BOARD BREAKS FOR LUNCH. IT
WILL END AROUND 2.00 PM.

FOR FURTHER INFORMATION:
Francis Beckett,
01 278 7801 Ex.46

Note that full information about the mass lobby is included

Speeches

The oldest form of press release is to distribute copies of speeches in advance. The Labour and Conservative press offices send out hundreds of speeches each year – thousands in an election year – to the media. Some trade-union leaders also like to get their message over via speeches which are released to the media in advance. It then becomes irrelevant how many people actually attend a meeting addressed by, say, Moss Evans – the rest of Britain can discover his thoughts or learn about a new political or trade-union initiative he wants to make by reading their papers or listening to the radio in the morning.

In a sense, the longest form of direct quote *is* the speech. But **journalists are not overkeen on speeches.** They prefer **people doing** things **rather than people saying** things. A speech will have to contain something newsworthy – a new announcement, a particularly sharp attack, fresh demands – to get reported. In any case, the journalist working on the story based on the speech will turn much of it into indirect speech, and will describe what was said and its import rather than report it directly.

A speech to a local meeting condemning the sale of locally manufactured goods to South Africa, even if crammed full of excellent comment and phrases that would bring forth cheers at a trade-union or Labour Party conference, will have little impact on the news editor's desk. 'Just another dose of some lefty mouthing off about South Africa again,' is likely to be the reaction, spoken or unspoken. If, however, the speech announces or calls for a demonstration or a picket or a stoppage involving the factory concerned, it then becomes a question of people *doing* (albeit potentially) rather than mere *talk*.

There is one big advantage in putting out speeches as press releases. If you have to prepare the speech or talk anyway, you might as well get it down on paper and arrange for a few copies to be sent off to the media. It can even be a time-saver if you know you have to give a report to a meeting on a particular problem and would like to get some media coverage. **If you are in a hurry or you cannot give enough time to preparing a news-story-style press release, you can send out the speech/report.**

If you do this, it is as well to add a short note on a separate piece of paper, summing up the main point of the speech in one sentence. For example:

In a report to the South London Labour Party last night

(Tuesday) local squatters' leader, John Brine, outlined new proposals to stop squatters being evicted by the GLC.

note to editors: the report in the form of the speech to the Labour Party is attached.

Even with a short speech it is as well to single out two or three of the main points and one or two quotes from the speech and include them in your accompanying note.

The embargo

The great advantage of press releases is that they can use the embargo system. This means that **you can send news to the media some time in advance of when you want it to appear.**

An obvious example is a speech to be made at a meeting. You send the speech in the form of a press release; but it would spoil the impact of the meeting if the contents of the speech were printed in the afternoon. So you write across the top of the press release 'NOT FOR USE UNTIL 8 P.M. TUESDAY 20 JANU-ARY' (or, more simply, 'EMBARGOED 8 p.m. 20 JAN'). Another example would be if you were planning a picket or demonstration which you wanted *both* to be a surprise *and* to have media coverage. In that case you could send out a press release with an embargo stating that the information should not be used until the time of the proposed event.

The embargo is most commonly used at national level when a complicated report is issued that will need some digesting. The accompanying press release is headed 'NOT FOR PUBLI-CATION UNTIL . . .' – the date being a few days in advance, so as to give journalists time to prepare in-depth reports, find illustrations and do background stories – none of which would be possible if the report had to be turned into a story as soon as it arrived in a newsroom. Government reports and white papers are nearly always sent out on this basis. Indeed many MPs, feeling tender about their parliamentary privilege, complain that journalists often have better advance – if confidential – access to important government publications than do MPs themselves.

A third use of the embargo is to try and control the timing of release of your news so as to secure coverage in particular media. Sunday is generally held to be a weak news day. Indi-viduals or organisations often embargo stories for Sunday, so that they stand a chance of getting used on Monday rather than

TRADES UNION CONGRESS
South East Regional Council

Chairman: J. Dunn   Secretary: JACK DROMEY

13 PLYMPTON ROAD, LONDON NW6 7EH
Telephone: 01-   (any time)

PRESS RELEASE: embargoed 0001 Monday 19th June 1978

SE TUC CALLS FOR EXTRA SUPPORT FOR GARNERS.

The SE TUC has written to all trade unions in London and the South East asking them to step up support for the pickets at Garner's restaurants.

In a letter to union branches the Secretary of the SE TUC, Jack Dromey says: 'Assistance is needed every lunchtime, in the evenings and at the weekend to picket those restaurants that are still open. Financial support for the strikers is also urgently required.'

Speaking about the call to increase the picketting Mr Dromey said: 'The mass tourist season is now in full swing. This is make or break time for the Garner's strike. I am especially keen for London trade unionists who speak a foreign language to come and help on the picket line by talking to tourists in their own language. So far a great number of tourists have refused to cross the picket line and gone to eat somewhere else but it would be helpful to explain the issue in their own language.'

The SE TUC together with the TGWU and the Greater London Association of Trades Councils is also organising a special conference on Garners which will be held at Transport House on Thursday 22nd June, 7.30 p.m.

For further information contact Jack Dromey

An example of the use of the embargo. Note also the strong quotes.

on the more competitive weekdays when courts, councils and parliaments are in action making news.

Timing an embargo needs careful thought. If you give a press release to regional newsrooms at 5.00 in the afternoon, it will be too late for the local evening paper and the regional television programmes. If you embargo it for 12.00 noon the next day, you will be likely to get more coverage from those two media but you may not get it in the local morning paper, nor on the breakfast-time local radio shows which is when local radio has its biggest audience. One approach is to embargo a story for 00.30 a.m.: that way you can hope to get coverage in the morning papers and on morning radio, but you may find the bigger-circulation evening paper ignoring the story because it has already appeared in the morning rival. A press release sent out on Tuesday but embargoed until Friday will win no friends in the local weekly paper – which prints on Wednesday and is published on Thursday, and might have given the biggest and best coverage of all to the story and so provided a signpost to other media to pick it up and use it.

Embargoes are a mixed blessing. They can be and are used cynically by management when a controversial decision is taken: the more newsworthy it is, the more they want to ensure that it is announced at the most advantageous time. In order to stop newsrooms basing the story on a tip-off or leak, they give it out confidentially on an embargo basis – thereby gaining time for themselves to pull together arguments and facts in the vital period between taking the decision and releasing it. Once the embargoed version of the story has arrived in the newsroom, journalists are reluctant to use it *even if they get the story from an independent source*, on the grounds that they would be thought (not so much by the firm as by other journalists) to be dishonouring the embargo.

Sometimes embargoes are used out of sheer spite against a particular newspaper. A particular firm may time its press releases always to give morning papers the news first, because it does not like the style of the evening paper; or perhaps a PRO has fallen out with a correspondent and times his or her embargoes to favour rival newspeople.

You cannot embargo an event. That is, you cannot announce in a press release that a meeting or a demonstration will take place at 8.00 p.m. but then place an embargo on the press release for midnight four hours later. **Radio and television have a right to use the news of the event from the moment it happens** (and that

```
PA
1 COAL (NOT FOR PUBLICATION BEFORE 1100 WEDNESDAY, JAN 24)
BY NICHOLAS TIMMINS, PA INDUSTRIAL CORRESPONDENT.
  THE MARKET FOR COAL IN BRITAIN WILL RISE BY AN ESTIMATED 40 PERCENT
BETWEEN NOW AND THE YEAR 2,000, THE NATIONAL COAL BOARD FORECAST
TODAY.
  THE BOARD TOLD THE COMMISSION ON ENERGY AND THE ENVIRONMENT,
WHICH HAS STARTED A STUDY ON THE LONG-TERM ENVIRONMENTAL IMP-
LICATION OF FUTURE COAL PRODUCTION AND USE, THAT THE MARKET FOR
COAL WAS LIKELY TO INCREASE FROM 122 MILLION TONNES TO 170 MILLION
TONNES BY THE END OF THE CENTURY AS OIL AND GAS BECOME SCARCER
AND MORE EXPENSIVE.
  POWER STATIONS WILL CONTINUE TO BE THE MOST IMPORTANT MARKET
CONSUMING AN ESTIMATED 90 MILLION TONNES BY 2,000, BECAUSE THE
NCB BELIEVES THE BURNING OF OIL IN POWER STATIONS WILL BECOME
INCREASINGLY UNDESIRABLE.
MF 0430 24/1 RFH NNN 1 COAL


2 COAL (SEE 11.00 HOURS WEDNESDAY EMBARGO)
  INDUSTRY'S REQUIREMENTS ARE EXPECTED TO GROW FASTEST - UP FROM
9 MILLION TONNES A YEAR NOW TO 40 MILLION BY 2,000 - ON THE BASIS
OF RISING OIL PRICES AND LESS GAS AVAILABLE FOR OTHER THAN PREMIUM
USES.
  COAL COULD AGAIN BECOME KING FOR A LARGE PART OF THE STEAM-
RAISING NEEDS OF INDUSTRY AND THE COAL BOARD IS CONVINCED THAT
NEW COMBUSTION TECHNIQUES WILL ENHANCE COAL'S COMPETITIVE POSITION
IN THIS MARKET.
  COAL WILL RETAIN ABOUT THE SAME SALES AS IT HAS NOW IN THE
DOMESTIC MARKET, WHILE A MODEST INCREASE IN STEEL PRODUCTION WILL
RETURN THE REQUIREMENT FOR COKING COAL TO THE LEVEL IT WAS AT
BEFORE THE STEEL RECESSION, THE NCB FORECASTS.
  THE BOARD SAYS IT IS ON TARGET TO MEET THE INCREASED DEMAND BY
SINKING NEW COLLIERIES AND EXTENDING EXISTING ONES.
MF 0430 24/1 RFH NNN 2 COAL


3 COAL (SEE 11.00 HOURS WEDNESDAY EMBARGO)
  BUT IT WARNED TODAY THAT WITHOUT CONTINUED HEAVY INVESTMENT
IN FURTHER COAL MINING CAPACITY THE INDUSTRY WOULD START DECLINING
AGAIN.
  AND DELAYS IN PLANNING APPLICATIONS FOR NEW MINES MIGHT AFFECT
THE RATE OF LONG-TERM EXPANSION.
END 0430 24/1 RFH NNN 3 COAL
```

The PA often transmits embargoed stories so that they can be set
up in type for a page that has to be designed early on in the
production schedule.

includes the contents of an embargoed speech from the moment it is made).

Do not over-use or abuse the embargo system. Journalists are not impressed by embargoes. PROs try to whip up interest over some unimportant bit of news by placing an embargo on it; and there is growing concern about the manipulative use of embargoes by some public bodies. Their use is best restricted to providing genuine advance notice so that stories can be prepared and written in good time. If you want to aim for a particular section of the media it is better to ensure delivery at the appropriate time – e.g., by issuing the press release at 4.00 p.m. for overnight coverage, rather than by an artificial embargo.

> The Greater London Council embargoed the embarrassing report on the inquiry into the controversy at the William Tyndale school for midnight one Friday. This meant, if the embargo was honoured, that London's two evening newspapers could not use the story until Monday, when it would be 'dead' journalistically. It also meant that it would get the relatively thin coverage of the Saturday editions of the national press.
>
> The *Evening Standard* decided to break the embargo and published full details on Friday afternoon. In this instance the paper was justified in its decision to ignore what was clearly a manipulative embargo.

In general, however, embargoes are firmly respected. As with off-the-record conversations (see page 122), there is far more you can let journalists know in confidence than is generally realised. Journalists have more to lose than they have to gain from abusing embargoes and publishing the odd advance story.

What a press release should look like

The appearance of a press release tells the journalist at a glance if it is going to help him or not. It should give a confident, easy-to-read impression and provide certain basic information in addition to the text of the release.

More important, a sub-editor has to be able to handle a press release with ease; she/he must have room to write in instructions to the printer or rewrite parts of the text. The more care taken over the presentation of a press release, the more chance of it being used with little alteration:

 ■ use headed notepaper
 ■ use a typewriter – and type neatly
 ■ put a date on the release

■ if you use an embargo, state your instructions in capital letters at the top of the release

■ always use double spacing: this allows the sub to re-write and insert instructions to the printer

■ type on one side of the paper only

■ use wide margins (about 1½ inches) on both sides of the paper – again, this is to let the sub write in instructions

■ use A4-size paper (the standard size for most office stationery)

■ never split a sentence over two pages: often, separate pages of a press release go to different printers for composition, so a split sentence can cause endless trouble

■ provide a simple heading at the top of the press release: this should not be a smart journalistic headline (leave that to the subs), but a short sentence that sums up the story

■ number the pages in a press release and give a catchline from Page 2 onwards*

■ if the press release covers more than one page, put at the bottom of each sheet the word 'More', or 'm.f.' ('more follows'), which are universally recognised terms indicating to both sub and printer that there is more to come

■ at the end of the text of a press release, put 'Ends' underneath and apart from the final sentence

■ *Always, always, always* put the name and telephone number (work and home) of the person who issued the release: journalists will not abuse home phone-numbers, but so much of their work, especially on an urgent story, is outside normal office hours that being able to make contact at home is vital

■ use staples rather than pins or paperclips

■ do not underline anything†

Different types of press release

News release. This is written in the style of a news story and should be complete and compact enough to be published as it is.

* The catchline is a key word from the heading, which enables subs and printers to identify *easily* to which story a piece of paper belongs. A press release whose heading is 'Overtime ban imposed at Rawlings' could have as its catchline on subsequent pages, 'Rawlings 2,' 'Rawlings 3,' etc.

† Underlining has a particular meaning for printers, and is used by sub-editors to indicate that a word or phrase should be printed in italics.

NEWS from NUPE

NATIONAL UNION OF PUBLIC EMPLOYEES
Civic House   Aberdeen Terrace   London SE3
Lee Green 2842

Public Relations & Research Officer: BERNARD DIX

For Immediate Release

NUPE ADOPTS NEW STRUCTURE

Britain's fifth largest union, the National Union of Public Employees, is to make sweeping changes in its organisation to give more effective power to rank and file members.

The changes were agreed at a special two-day conference when more than 500 delegates considered a report on reorganisation presented by the Union's Executive Council.

Under the new rules adopted at the conference the local strength of the Union will be concentrated on district committees consisting of stewards and branch secretaries. Above these will be area committees and divisional councils which will also consist of stewards and branch secretaries.

At national level four committees of rank and file members will specialise in the main service interests of the Union; local government, the National Health Service, universities and water service.

The Union's Executive Council will be increased by ten members to 26. Five of the new seats will be open to women members only. The Executive will set up economic, organisation development and finance committees to deal in detail with major subject items.

The new structure, which was drawn up by the Executive Council after they had studied a report prepared for them by the Department of Sociology at the University of Warwick, provides interconnecting links between the various levels of Union organisation.

When opening the conference the Union's President, Mr John New, said: 'We are living in a period of rapid social, economic and political change. Our task is to decide how to adapt our Union not just to meet those changes, but so that we can force them into directions which will benefit our members and the working class in general.

'We are not reorganising just for the sake of doing something different, we are reorganising so that we can use the full potential strength of our Union in the year ahead of us.'

ENDS

A background press release. It is doubtful if much of it would be carried by the media, but if nothing else it tells specialist reporters about a new structure.

Background release. This is to provide detailed information for journalists from which they can cull information for their own stories or which they can file away for future use. A background release might be used for giving the statistical basis for a claim or report.

Press statement. This is a release giving a precise statement or quote and nothing more (the text of a speech can count as a long press statement). A common use arises during or at the end of negotiations, when both sides agree a statement which is jointly released without extra explanation.

Letter release. This is the text of a letter written to someone. It is a useful device to convey a message. The press release simply reads:

In a letter to the Prime Minister/Managing Director/ General Secretary shop stewards at Smithings have asked/ called for/demanded his/her resignation/dismissal. The letter is attached.

In every situation when you want media coverage you can send a letter to someone outlining the points you want to make and then release the letter as a press release.

Written article. This is not really a press release at all. You can write your own piece for a newspaper or magazine and submit it for publication. Pick up the style and length from whatever publication you are aiming at and have a go. **If it is well written on a local subject of interest and you are an appropriate person to comment** there is a good chance that it may be used. All the usual rules about clear writing, avoiding jargon, and professional layout apply.

Examples

The first example below is taken from COHSE's *Union Stewards' Handbook*, and shows the same story presented badly and presented well. The following three Examples refer to made-up situations involving fictitious unions and individuals; but they show the flow of a good press release, the value of using **strong quotes** and adding a **note to the picture editor,** and **sensible use of embargoes.**

34 Birmingham Street

Hazeltown

1492 branch had a meeting yesterday in the small common room of
the old wing of the hospital and much business was discussed.
Mr. Johnson asked about the delay in the ASC bonus scheme and
Mr. Robinson told him that Mr. Carruthers seemed to be unduly
delaying the matter. After lengthy discussion it was resolved:
  'in the light of the incredible delay in getting management
  to move on this scheme that the Regional Secretary be contacted
  and that we write to management telling them that the whole
  branch was very angry and that there was likely to be trouble
  if nothing had happened by the next meeting.'
The Chairman had previously welcomed a lot of new members to the
meeting.

Bad

(Fictitious)

Press Release: 26 February 1978   Hazeltown Branch

COHSE GETS TOUGH ON BONUS SCHEME

At a packed meeting last night (25 Feb) the Hazeltown branch of COHSE
decided to issue a strong warning to local management about a seven-year
delay in implementing a bonus scheme.

One hundred members heard Branch Secretary, John Robinson, describe
the delay in bonus pay for the ancillary staff as 'incredible and
totally unjustified'.

After the meeting Mr. Robinson said, 'We are standing by our part of
the bargain: it is over six weeks since our last correspondence with
the Area Personnel Office. Our record recruiting in the last month
shows that all the staff are very angry and support our lead in this.

'I shall be having urgent discussions with the Regional Office. I'm
afraid this constitutes what looks like an ultimatum for industrial
action.

'Management has until 15 March - the next branch meeting - to persuade
us that they really want to resolve the matter'.

COHSE has 165,000 members in the National Health Service.

                                ENDS

For further information contact: John Robinson
                            Tel: 278456 (home)
                                   84763 ext 42, 44 (work)

Good

(Fictitious)

NATIONAL UNION OF BUILDING WORKERS

Press Release: immediate

SHEFFIELD BRANCH
Trade and Labour Hall
Park Road, Sheffield 9

16 June

DEATH TOLL MUST STOP

Building workers in Sheffield are calling for sweeping new
safety measures to be introduced following the death of three of
their colleagues on the Sheffield Civic Centre development last
week.

They want full-time union safety convenors to be appointed on
all sites where more than £50,000-worth of work is being carried
out.

The 3,000-strong Sheffield branch of the National Union of Building
Workers is pressing the union executive to include the call for
safety convenors when they meet the Building Employers Federation
in London next Tuesday (20 June).

'There are three local families who would not be mourning their
lost fathers if employers would pay some attention to safety',
said NUBW branch chairman, John Wilson.

n.f.

'There are masses of regulations governing safety in the building industry as well as major legislation like the 1974 Health and Safety at Work Act. But all this counts for nothing if there is not someone on the site charged with making sure the safety rules are obeyed.

'We want to see safety convenors appointed from amongst the workforce on each big site. It might seem expensive at first sight to have a man full-time on safety but we reckon it would save money in three ways:

* fewer stoppages in production because of accidents

* better and quicker jobs as men worked more confidently

* less pressure on local ambulances and hospitals

'Building employers are so short-sighted in their chase for profit', said Mr. Wilson.

The building workers' demand comes against a mounting background of deaths and injuries in the construction industry. 142 building workers were killed last year and more than 2,000 injured. In Sheffield alone there were six deaths and 267 reported injuries.

'None of the public seems to care if a building worker dies', said Mr. Wilson. 'If a policeman gets killed or fishermen are drowned or there is a tragedy in a mine it merits front-page news and immediate attention from the politicians and the public.

m.f.

'A building worker is killed every fourteen hours on average in Britain and yet there is no outcry, only their families and workmates are left to mourn them', he added.

As well as pressure on employers   the Sheffield branch of the NUBW also want the government to tighten up building safety rules and they are going to ask the city council not to award contracts to building firms with poor safety records.

'At the end of the day this slaughter - and that's what it is - will stop when employers are forced to take safety more seriously and put a greater priority on human life than on profit.

'The appointment of safety convenors would only add an infinitesimal amount to the cost of building and in the long run would save money.

'If the government and the employers' federation won't act we shall have to take matters into our own hands'.

ENDS

Contact: John Wilson   Tel: Sheffield 00894 (work)
                                            02267 (home)

Note to Picture Editors:

We can arrange for the widow of Tom Kelly, one of the dead men, to be pictured at the site of the accident. She is also willing to be interviewed about her attitudes on safety in the industry.

(Fictitious)

NATIONAL ASSOCIATION OF SUPERVISORS

Press release: immediate   NAS House
                                             Devon Street
17 November 1978   Leicester

To: All East Midlands media   Tel: Leicester 01578

n.b. Picture of Peter Curran supplied on request

NEW NAS ORGANISER FOR EAST MIDLANDS

The National Association of Supervisors has appointed a new organiser
to cover the East Midlands. He is Peter Curran, currently Chairman
of the NAS Midlands Regional Council and a senior supervisor with
the Gas Board.

The new appointment reflects the growth of light industry and office
work in the East Midlands with many white-collar supervisors and junior
managers still not organised in any union.

'NAS has doubled its membership in the past ten years and there is
tremendous potential in this area', said Mr. Curran.

39-year-old Mr. Curran is married with 3 children. His wife, Anne,
is a social worker with Leicestershire County Council. Born in Derby
he now lives in Market Harborough and will work from NAS House in
Leicester. Mr. Curran has been a member of the NAS national executive
council since 1971 and is currently secretary of the East Midlands TUC
Regional Council. His hobbies include walking, reading political
novels and raising money for MIND, the mental health charity.

'NAS is delighted to have secured Peter Curran as an official', said
NAS General Secretary, Clive Harrod. 'He will open up the benefits
of trade unionism to thousands of supervisors in the East Midlands'.

                              ENDS

Contact: Peter Curran   Tel: 0186 95348 (home)

(Fictitious)

Press Release: strictly embargoed
1p.m. Friday, May 2

SOUTHAMPTON
TRADES
COUNCIL

MASS PICKET FOR ARGENTINIAN AMBASSADOR'S VISIT

The Argentinian ambassador in London will have a surprise reception
when he turns up as the guest of the Southampton chamber of commerce
on Friday (2nd May).

250 local trade unionists plan to picket the city hotel
(Queen's, Eccles Square) where he will be speaking, in protest at the
repression of human rights in Argentina.

The demonstration, which is expected to attract students from local
colleges, has been organised by Southampton Trades Council.

Trades Council secretary, Malcolm Brown, said: 'Argentina is now
recognised as one of the most brutal and repressive countries in the
world.

'US Secretary of State, Cyrus Vance, has compiled a list of 7,000 people
who have disappeared. Many of them are trade unionists, which is why
Southampton Trades Council is concerned.

'The docks here are the channel through which much of the trade between
Britain and Argentina flows. We are not objecting to that trade but
we cannot allow the representative of this murderous regime to believe
that the ordinary people of Southampton welcome his presence.'

Since the military take-over in Argentina in March 1976 there has been
wide-spread torture and detention without trial. Amnesty International,
the Nobel Peace Prize winning organisation, has detailed the tortures
and repression. One wife of a trade unionist was found dying by the
roadside with her breast almost torn off.

m.f.

'We are particularly concerned that Argentina is trying to put on an
attractive face to the outside world as the World Cup will be staged
there later this year. Hitler used the 1936 Olympic Games as propaganda
for his rule of terror in Nazi Germany and the thugs now bossing
Argentina hope the World Cup will do a similar public relations job
for their repressive regime', said Mr. Brown.

Southampton Trades Council has also written to the Foreign Secretary,
Dr. David Owen, asking him to ensure that the Scottish Football
Association is made aware of the torture and terror inside Argentina.
Malcolm Brown, himself a Scot from Kilmarnock, hopes that Scotland
wins the World Cup, in fact he's sure they will, but not at the price
of promoting the Argentinian regime.

'We want to tell the ambassador that he cannot use football to
disguise torture. In our small way we shall be blowing the whistle
in protest at one of the biggest fouls against a country's people
ever committed.'

ENDS

For further information please contact: Malcolm Brown at 02157 ext 43
                                          or at home   021469

Note to Editors: full details of general and individual repression
and torture in Argentina can be obtained from Amnesty International,
London.

6.

Pictures

Picture ideas / mugshots and wallpaper

'A picture is worth a thousand words.' This is one of journalism's oldest sayings.

Newspaper **picture editors** are important figures. They have to be persuaded **independently of news editors** that a photographer should be sent out. They also like to initiate coverage of events in which the photograph itself tells the story.

> In the 1978–79 NUJ provincial journalists' strike, members at York decided to set up a picket on the River Ouse. The picture of a striking journalist holding up a placard in a rowing boat was used nationally and on local television.

> At the height of the controversy inside the National Union of Mineworkers over the introduction of productivity payments, a group of Yorkshire miners – unhappy about what they saw to be a lack of militant leadership from the NUM President – sent Joe Gormley a present. It was a miner's shovel. Attached to it was a label suggesting that Gormley might like to come back to a pit and dig some coal himself before he chose to ditch the miners' overall pay demand and go for productivity payments instead. It was a bitter, angry time for the NUM but the widely published picture of Gormley's shovel said more about the Yorkshire miners' attitude than a 10,000 word article could ever have done.

> As part of the campaign to highlight repression in Argentina, the former Wolves and Northern Ireland footballer, and Chairman of the Professional Footballers Association Derek Dougan, was pictured handing in to the Argentine embassy a football covered with the names of some of the dead, tortured, missing and exiled people of the country.

There is an element of artificiality, of showmanship, in thinking up and **staging** good visual events. If a picture is going to be noticed by the picture editor and published, and if it is to remain in the mind of the reader or viewer, it will have to be **out of the ordinary.** And that means that people will have to *do* something, or pose in a manner that is not ordinary.

News photographers are professional journalists, who will chivvy or re-position their subjects to get the most effective picture. Sometimes it will be obvious – like asking picketing strikers to move a few yards so that they can be photographed standing under the company sign. Sometimes it will be a necessary re-staging of an event – like asking a meeting to raise hands in a vote a second time because the cameras were not ready when the vote proper was taken. It may involve asking a worker to be pictured with his tools, or, say, sitting in his cab rather than standing alone. Usually these suggestions from the photographer will make for a better picture.

But be careful of any attempt to manipulate. A picture of TGWU pickets in the 1979 road haulage dispute was taken with the camera facing the sun so that the pickets came over as darkly anonymous sinister forces.

If the picture editor can be confident that the picture illustrating the story will be out of the ordinary – **because you have told the picture desk in advance** – there is more chance of a photographer being sent.

Picture ideas

■ always make placards and banners with simple, clear, dark lettering on a light background so that the message or slogan comes over clearly in a photograph

■ children in a picture always command attention

■ refuse collectors on strike will create a better picture if they are photographed behind a long line of dustbins

■ teachers can bring out a blackboard to do a simple public lesson on why class sizes should be cut down

■ a civil servant in pin-stripes and bowler with brolly and briefcase and carrying a placard will almost guarantee a published picture – if he wore his normal jumper and jeans there would be far less interest

■ offer to arrange a photo-call at the home of a striking worker where she can be interviewed with her husband and children

■ in a low-wage dispute, suggest that the photographer take a close-up picture of a wage-slip

■ to highlight poor facilities, make a huge soap-powder

(Fictitious)

U N I O N   O F   H A R D   W O R K E R S

98 Green Road
Ayr

18 February 1978

Press Release: <u>embargoed</u>
10a.m. Tuesday, February 21

CHILDREN WEARING DUNCES CAPS TO HAND IN PETITION FOR NEW SCHOOL

A group of forty children accompanied by their parents will hand in
a petition at the Town Hall next Tuesday (21 Feb) at 10a.m. calling
for a new primary school to be built on the Keir Hardie estate.
The children will wear dunces caps as their comment on the difficulties
the local council place in the way of primary school education on
the giant estate.
The petition, which has 1,500 signatures, has been organised by local
parents and the Union of Hard Workers, many of whose members live on
the estate.
UHW Regional Secretary, Harry Ashton, said 'These children have further
to go to school than my members have to go to work.'

ENDS

Contact: Harry Ashton   Tel: 98006 (office) or 00917 (home)
Note to Picture Editors: The children will be outside the Town Hall
from 9.45. As well as the dunces caps they will be carrying protest
placards.

This press release has a note giving special advice of a possible
picture.

packet, marked *Brand X*, and present it to the management with the suggestion that they clean up the place

■ hand out leaflets on buses or trains or outside schools or hospital gates whenever there is a public-service dispute

■ when handing in a petition, arrange for a large group to go along to the town hall, company office or union head-quarters and, if possible, see if someone will agree to accept the petition at the front door.

Mugshots and wallpaper

Most of the pictures used in newspapers, and most of the film broadcast in television news bulletins, is **undramatic material used to illustrate the written story.** The national politician making a speech, the burned-out building, a queue of traffic, snow-covered fields – all these are standard pictures to cover a story. In television, the kind of basic 'shot' (of, say, a Longbridge factory or a pit-head) that is used for a story about a dispute is referred to as **wallpaper** – that is, it covers visually, in a **genera-lised** way, the specific story being reported.

Look through any newspaper – *The Guardian*, the *Daily Mail*, the *Kidderminster Shuttle* – and there will be a larger number of people's faces, about one or two inches square. These are called **mugshots** in journalist jargon, and are used like headlines and other typographical devices to break up the grey-ness of a page. That is the main reason for their use, although in formal terms they do illustrate the person or persons named in the text of the story.

In any story longer than a couple of paragraphs, most papers – especially local weekly and small evening papers – will use a small picture showing the face or head and shoulders of the people featured. But they can only use a mugshot if they have one on file, and photographers can't be expected to have taken a picture of *everyone* who might suddenly be needed for a story.

Very often, company or corporation PROs will send in a stock picture with their press releases (even if it isn't used with that particular story, the picture is filed for future use). Famous people like the Queen, Len Murray, Brian Clough or Arthur Scargill do not have to send in their own pictures, but if you are trying to initiate news coverage you should **let the local news-papers have a picture of the individual mentioned in your press release.**

It may feel big-headed and a bit silly to send in a picture of yourself. But all you are doing is making the sub-editor's job easier (by giving him an extra element to play with in designing the page layout) and giving yourself the chance of a marginal increase in the **impact** of the story if readers can see your face smiling out of the page.

However, **the pictures have to be good.** Holiday snaps, or pictures taken by a friend with an Instamatic, *will not do.*

■ If you have established friendly contact with journalists on your **local paper,** you can ask one of the photographers to do you a favour and take and print pictures of you. With darkroom facilities in every newspaper this can be done easily enough. It will help the transaction if you offer something to the photographer in return – after all, you are having a slice of his professional time.

■ If you prefer, you can go to a **professional high-street photographer** (and have your picture taken and the required number of prints made). This will be more expensive, but for a new full-time official who is moving into an area it is a worthwhile one-off union expense.

■ Alternatively, since photography is one of the Britain's most popular hobbies, any large trade-union branch, political party or local pressure group should have at least one keen **amateur photographer** who can be asked (perhaps for a small honorarium) to take people's pictures for circulation to the local papers.

Most mainstream newspapers will accept mugshots from almost any source, provided that they are technically acceptable photographs (and printed 6″ × 4″ on glossy paper). But they tend to be suspicious of amateur photographs of events or situations. **Socialist newspapers, on the other hand, welcome pictures of all kinds.** With very stretched resources, *Socialist Worker* or *Labour Weekly* simply cannot send a photographer to the many socialist or trade-union news events that happen each week.

■ Many **local art colleges and polytechnics** run full-time courses for would-be photographers. Individual lecturers and sympathetic students can be asked to come and take photographs of a particular event (you can find out names by contacting the secretary of the students union or one of the left-wing societies at the college). In a long-running campaign or dispute, this can provide an excellent source of imaginative photographs for use in the left-wing and trade-union press. You can also ask for the prints to be enlarged and put up on notice boards at the dispute headquarters.

■ There is now a growing body of **freelance photographers** who specialise in taking pictures of left-wing and trade-union events and selling them to appropriate newspapers and magazines (their names are usually printed in tiny print alongside the picture when it is published). Several of them are connected with a socialist trade-union oriented, freelance photo agency called *Report* (411 Oxford Street, London W1: 01-493-7737) which has a good reputation in the left-wing and trade-union press for pictures connected with socialist or workers' stories. If they agree with your estimation of the importance of the event, they will come and take a picture and sell it to as many newspapers as possible.

7.

News conferences

How to organise a news conference / when
and why you should hold a news conference

Holding a news or press conference is a way of getting
journalists from the different media to come in a body to *you*.

Few press releases can contain *everything* you want to say.
Besides, journalists will probably have questions to put to you
on the basis of whatever statement or announcement you have
made. Holding a news conference allows you and the journalists
to get together in person. It also allows more than one person to
speak and answer questions on behalf of the organisation holding
the news conference. A news conference also brings all the
journalists to the same place at the same time so that no journalist or newsroom feels excluded. For photographers and broadcasting reporters, it guarantees the physical presence of a person
to be interviewed or photographed.

A news conference is an 'event', and newsrooms like events.
It is written down in the news diary and, depending on the
strength of the story and on the pressure of the day's other news,
the news editor may arrange for it to be covered. The very act of
organising and holding a news conference is a kind of signal to
the news editor that there is likely to be something useful to be
gained.

How to organise a news conference

When you compose your announcement of a news conference, follow the rules for press releases. You must tell the
newsrooms **where** it will be, **when** it will take place, **what** it is
about, **who** will be speaking and **why** you are calling it. Do tell
them what is going to be said (but place an embargo on it until
the time of the news conference): some newsrooms will un-
avoidably not be able to send a reporter along, and there is no

reason why the main point of the news to be announced at the press conference should be kept secret.

■ The best time to hold a news conference is between 10.15 a.m. and 11.30 a.m. Television newsrooms tend not to get going until about 10.00 a.m. and evening newspapers become fidgety about deadlines after 12.00 noon.

■ You should hold it in a suitable room with enough chairs set out. Sometimes a press conference will attract no more than a reporter from the local weekly and one from the local freelance agency. If it's a big story running in the national news, you may find 20 or more journalists turning up.

■ The people who are the subject of the press conference should sit facing the journalists, preferably (although not absolutely necessarily) behind a table.

■ Copies of the press release/statement/speech and/or any other relevant documents should be available. Journalists like to have a piece of paper with the raw facts or announcement on it, and it helps them to have something to refer to when asking supplementary questions.

■ Everyone should be introduced, and you should ask the journalists to give their names and say which organisations they represent when they ask questions. This helps to make a personal link between you and the journalists – you can refer to them by name when answering questions. Also, if the worst happens and the report produced from the news conference is inaccurate or biased, you have a record of the individual responsible.

■ A cup of coffee goes down well, and so too does a warm room. Big companies sometimes lay on incredibly lavish press conferences, with smoked-salmon lunches and free briefcases full of PR propaganda. Journalists like the free booze but are correctly cynical about the motives behind such generosity. Workers and trade unions need not go to those lengths; but if you have invited a journalist to attend your press conference it is because you want the publicity, and the least you can do, as you would for any other invited guest is to treat him or her with courtesy and ensure that he/she is reasonably comfortable.

■ A news conference **should not take long**. About half an hour is enough to cover most subjects (but remember to allow time for all the comings and goings).

Radio and television reporters will need somewhere quiet to do an interview after the press conference itself. It is extremely difficult to conduct an interview for these media during the course of an ordinary press conference. It may be a bore to have to go over the same points to two or three different people armed with microphones, but this nuisance is dictated by the way broadcasters have to work (see the section on *film interviews* in Chapter 9).

When and why should you hold a news conference

It really is a matter of individual judgement. Trivial news items, worth only a couple of paragraphs in the local weekly, do not justify a news conference. **There should always be a good story from the journalist's point of view.** The region's annual report (with details of strikes and pay increases), for example, or an important new appointment, do justify a news conference so that further comments can be made.

Sometimes press conferences can be organised very quickly. If you know there is to be a crucial meeting which will take an important decision, you can telephone the key local media and say that you will hold a press conference half an hour after the meeting is over, when you will announce the result and comment on it. This can save the messy jostling around an entrance as reporters push and shove to try and get a reply – you say to them, 'I'm sorry, I'll talk to you all in 20 minutes at the Labour Hall.' It also means that other shop stewards can attend, to explain the meeting's decision.

You don't always have to give advance notice. During a newsworthy trial, tribunal hearing, negotiating meeting or public inquiry, journalists can be told even at the last minute that a news conference will be held at such-and-such a place half an hour after it ends. As well as giving them a fixed time when they know comment will be available, this also gives you a little time in which to collect your thoughts before making a public comment on the outcome. Be flexible, however, if a journalist pleads that the deadline will be missed (for example, a radio reporter whose main news bulletin is due between the end of the event and the scheduled start-time of the news conference) and do a quick interview on the spot.

If you are involved in a major dispute which is attracting daily national-news attention, you should try, as far as possible, to control the news approach by holding a daily news conference at a regular time. You may not be able to avert or correct inaccuracies, but at least the reporters covering the story will have no excuse for not knowing what your comments are on the developing situation.

During the Grunwick mass picketing, the strike committee and
local trades council held a press conference at a fixed time –
11.15 a.m. – every morning. Overall, the news coverage of
Grunwick was distorted in favour of the management and the
police. But the technique of holding the daily press conference
at least allowed the strikers and the trades-council secretary,
Jack Dromey, to make forceful comments on the day's events.
All the reporters had to attend in case they missed an important announcement, and the country's evening papers, desperate
for any quotes or comments from Grunwick, were happy to
print whatever was said (a report was sent out daily on the PA
telex to evening paper newsrooms everywhere). Dromey and
the strike committee realised that what he said would always
take second place beside the general line about police/picket
violence that dominated the Grunwick coverage, but at least
Dromey was making himself available and ensuring that the
reporters did have quotes about police brutality and in support
of the strikers' case. The strikers and pickets were bitterly
angry, and justifiably so, at some of the disgracefully unfair
reporting of the Grunwick mass picket, but Dromey and the
strike committee wisely swallowed their anger enough to go on
holding the daily conference. Even if the newspapers did not
print their comments fully, at least the journalists would not
have the excuse that no-one was willing to talk to them about
the strikers' point of view.

Compare this with the unofficial action by power workers
in autumn 1977. This led to blackouts and tremendous press
interest – but the unofficial strike committee would not be interviewed and tried to remain anonymous. It is certainly true that
news coverage was bound to be hostile because of the disruption
caused, and because the action was unofficial. But by not talking,
and trying to remain anonymous (the secrecy was relative – the
men's unions, employers, and local communities knew who they
were), the workers missed a chance to put over their case and
explain why they felt driven to take action. Holding a daily news
conference would not have won the media over to the side of the
workers. But ITN and BBC TV News and all the press would
show interviews *explaining* the grievance, instead of relying on
employers, politicians and other bureaucrats, all of whom
wanted to see the strike defeated.

Contrast that, in turn, with the skill with which the EEPTU
General Secretary, Frank Chapple (not a man with a very high
regard for journalists), used the media when he was presenting
the electricity unions' official pay claim in spring 1978. In an
attempt to soften up the employers and the government, and at
the same time present a militant face to his own members at a
time of increasing internal criticism about his style of right-wing

Press needs better PR

IT IS REALLY not surprising that some of the union's members in Fleet Street get a "bad press" when they are involved in disputes.

I have had the doubtful privilege of covering the two recent journalists' disputes at the *Daily Mirror* and the *Sun* for ITN. In 14 years of industrial reporting I have seldom met a more un-cooperative group of trade unionists than our membership in these two papers. And I have met some pretty un-cooperative trade unionists in that time.

Almost any request for information about the NUJ's case is greeted with a refusal ranging from simple discourtesy to outright rudeness. These "brothers" seem to assume that the main aim of ITN NUJ members is to attack the NUJ's case. As ITN's FoC, chairman of the union's London TV branch, and as a member of the Broadcasting Industrial Council, I would have thought my track record might have persuaded them otherwise. But no. Their outright refusal to say anything about their case — often doupled with a suggestion to go away (but not in those words) — leaves ITN with no alternative but to report the story in a one-sided way. And then they blame us for reporting only the management side!!

What on earth do these "elite" of journalism, these "communicators," think they stand to gain from their refusal to communicate and their arrogant discourtesy? One can only assume their case is such a bad one, they dare not put it.

GILES SMITH,
London TV.

Letter in *The Journalist*, the NUJ journal, September 1978.

leadership, he granted interviews and made strong comments on doorsteps all over the place. Neither Chapple nor the unofficial power-workers' leaders *like* journalists. But he knew how to use the media. The power workers did not.

Such dramatic industrial action aside, you may find yourself holding a press conference to which *no one* turns up. Alternatively, friendly reporters may come along, chat endlessly and swig your coffee – and then nothing appears in the paper.

Don't worry. You *may* have misjudged the news strength of the story, but what is more likely is that some other story had just broken and diverted your reporters (or crowded out their

report of your press conference when the chief sub made his final
decision about what was to appear on the page).

In 1973, a campaign was launched in Moseley to get a private
park opened for public use. Two mothers whose children had
nowhere to play chained themselves to the park railings,
dressed up as suffragettes. It was a good news event and advance
press releases had been sent out. Yet no reporter or photographer turned up. The reason? A bomb had gone off in the city
forty minutes before the embargoed news event and every
newsroom dropped all planned coverage to report the
explosion.

(Fictitious)

LEEDS ANTI-NAZI LEAGUE

Embargoed: Noon 29th January   C/o Labour Club
                                                    Leeds 8

TO ALL NEWS EDITORS

NEWS CONFERENCE TO ANNOUNCE LEEDS ANTI-NAZI CARNIVAL

Your are invited to a News Conference to be held at Leeds Labour
Club at 11 a.m. on Monday 29 January, when details will be revealed
of a major carnival to be organised the following weekend (Sat 3
February) in Leeds.

Peter Hain, national Press Officer of the Anti-Nazi League, will
be at the press conference as will local organisers and Leeds
councillors.

The carnival will take the form of a short rally followed by a
march – with colourful floats – to Roundhay Park. Full details
will be given at the news conference.

For more information contact: J. Smith   Tel: Leeds 98765

This press release sets out the style for announcing a news
conference.

There are cases where it is extremely constructive to have held a news conference and talked to reporters *even if* nothing appears in the papers. The TUC's practice is a good example. Every month the TUC's General Council meets. The news value of the meetings varies. Sometimes the General Council will take a decision on a matter of great public interest; sometimes the meeting ends without any but routine, humdrum matters having been discussed. Yet the TUC holds a press conference for industrial reporters after *each* meeting – no matter what the news value – and the TUC General Secretary comes along and chats with reporters. For both the journalists and the TUC it does not really matter if the General Council meeting provides news or not. The news conference maintains contacts at a personal level between Len Murray and the TUC press officer and the journalists. It also gives the journalists a chance to question Murray in person about some point that is not formally connected with the General Council's business. The whole exercise, whether or not there is a page lead for the next day, helps to oil the connection that the TUC has built up with the corps of national industrial reporters.

8.

Dealing with journalists

Making contact / what to say

Making contact

Establishing relationships with individual journalists

Far better than sending off letters and press releases or phoning up newsrooms out of the blue is to have a personal relationship with a journalist who can be approached direct.

No-one can know personally every reporter and sub-editor on every newspaper or television station, but an effort can be made to contact a correspondent who specialises in the subject area in which you have an interest.

Look through the *Guardian* or *Daily Telegraph* and you will see individual correspondents covering such fields as:

- labour (i.e. trade unions) – sometimes referred to as the industrial correspondent
- education
- health services
- local government
- planning
- agriculture.

On evening papers outside London, there may not be this range of correspondents, but there will usually be a labour or industrial correspondent covering trade-union stories and a municipal correspondent covering stories connected with the council; on evening papers in bigger cities, there may also be an education and health correspondent.

The national television and radio newsrooms have specialised correspondents too; but, in most English regional television stations and on local radio stations, the small number of reporters employed have to turn their hands on a day to day basis to whatever story comes up.

Some general reporters concentrate on certain types of stories. Martin Walker of the *Guardian*, for example, has covered most of that paper's stories on the National Front.

Having identified a named journalist you should try to meet him or her, or at least have a long talk over the phone (the best way of doing this is to have a story which you think will be of interest). At best, ask to meet the reporter near his or her office for a chat; at worst, turn up unannounced – it's a rare newsman who won't see you for five minutes.

On first meeting the reporter, state candidly that you are interested in getting wider and better coverage of your union's or organisation's activities and want to find out how you can best fit in with the requirements of the newsroom concerned.

These are the main points you should cover:

■ what kind of stories do they require?

■ would a weekly call to discuss what's going on in your field help?

■ give them details about the structure of the local set-up, and the names and telephone-numbers of suitable contacts

■ find out what their time schedules are, including the latest time for accepting news and any preferences for getting material well in advance of publication date

■ ask if they have photographs in their files of leading local trade-union spokesmen and if necessary offer to arrange a convenient date for the photographers to come round to photograph your colleagues

■ explain any particular difficulties you have as far as contacting the media is concerned, and give times when you will be away from a telephone (if possible, nominate someone to take messages for you).

The value of **personal contact** with individual journalists cannot be over-stressed. The level of approach will, of course, vary. Editors of big evening papers, for example, are far less likely to be available than the editor of a small weekly. On local radio stations, ask to see the news editor; he usually has considerable control over what is covered. But any news editor will listen more carefully to what one of his reporters says – **so make every effort to cultivate journalists, whatever their position.**

When you are phoning a newsroom to establish a general introduction, think about the best **time** to do it. Most newsrooms have easy times of the day when the pressure is lower – 11.30–1.00 for morning papers, after 3.00 on evening papers and three hours before the transmission time of the main news programmes for radio and television stations.

Contacting journalists to make a specific point

It is extremely valuable to have established relationships with individual journalists, but you will also sometimes need to contact newsrooms out of the blue – to make a statement, or swiftly to get over your side of a story if an unbalanced report has appeared (see Chapter 12 for the different question of registering a complaint or seeking a formal correction).

Try always to get through to the reporter who is responsible for the story you are reacting to. Say who you are and that you have a short statement about the issue. Have this written down – at least in note form – beforehand, so as not to waste their time or yours. If the reporter is not available ask to speak to the news editor; he or she may pass you on to another reporter who will take down your points, but you will at least have lodged in his or her mind the fact that you are trying to give the newsroom your facts and opinions on the story.

You can suggest to the reporters on the bigger newsdesks (e.g., national newsrooms and big regional newspapers and broadcasting newsrooms) that you 'put your statement over to copy': this means acting virtually as a journalist, dictating a short report to a copytaker. For this you must have the statement ready – written out in the same form as a press release. However, shortness is vital here. The copytaker will be annoyed if it is more than 250–300 words and the newsdesk will be extremely annoyed if the copy-phones are clogged up for any length of time. Always provide a contact telephone-number when you give a statement to copy.

If you already have an individual contact in the newsroom, always try to speak to that particular journalist. They may pass you on to another journalist, but you may get some advice first on how best to make your point.

Always remember that a news editor or correspondent who gets approached by a *colleague* with a new fact or further statement will pay more attention, as one professional to another, than if a strange voice is talking down the telephone.

Contacting the Press Association

The best way of circulating a statement to all the national and evening papers and broadcasting newsrooms is to get it on to the PA. The PA has the same range of specialist correspondents as a big national newspaper, and you can ask specifically for, say, the industrial 'desk' or the education correspondent. You can also talk to someone on the newsdesk who will take down details of any story and possibly write it up. A newsdesk reporter may ask that you put a statement over to copy. This is quite common, as the PA takes a large number of statements from organisations and individuals.

It is possible to bypass the newsdesk at the PA and give a statement *direct* to copy. Simply ring the PA (01-353-7440), ask confidently for copy – just say 'copy'. A copytaker will come on. Say who you are and whom you represent and that you want to put over a short statement. The copytaker will ask for a contact telephone-number. Give the statement. Every minute or so, the copytaker will say 'turning' (when a new sheet of copy paper is being inserted). Wait a second and the copytaker will say, 'ready' – and off you go again. The PA puts out an enormous amount of news, and prides itself on the width of its coverage. None the less, the PA newsdesk will not be very pleased with a statement arriving *via* copy about an issue which would only merit a small story in a weekly paper; so **try to reserve direct statements to PA copy for comments on what is already a big running story.**

Contact lists

As well as giving individual reporters your telephone-numbers, home and work, it is a useful idea to send to all newsrooms a list of names, with details about the various people's responsibilities and titles in the organisation. This can be done at the beginning of each year, or after the annual meeting when new officers are elected.

Contact telephone-numbers are vital, including home telephone-numbers (see pages 3 and 86 for the need to provide vide home telephone-numbers).

It is best to send out this annual contact list with a press release containing a story, or else to issue it when you hold your **annual media briefing** (see below).

Annual media briefing

At the beginning of each year, or at the time the annual report is published, a union should hold a briefing for journalists. This is **best done at city, county or regional level**. You won't get a journalist from Granada Television, based in Manchester, to go to Bolton for a briefing meeting of the Bolton branch of a union – if he/she went to Bolton, he/she would have to go to all other towns in the North West where union branches or shop-stewards' committees were holding such briefings, and would never get any work done! It is best for **regional** trade-union machinery to be used, because news editors, industrial correspondents and reporters can then be invited from a fairly wide area.

The object of the briefing meeting is two-fold.

Firstly, it enables you to **introduce the various trade-union officials,** lay and full-time, **who can be contacted during the year,** and **provide the journalists with an up-to-date picture of union strength in the region** (where the membership is, the main employers dealt with, the current structure in the area, where the decision-making power lies and the relationship between the local trade-union structure and the national organisation).

Secondly, it enables you to **present journalists with your idea of likely developments** in the twelve months ahead, **and any specific plans or campaigns** you have in mind.

You can outline the union's position on:

■ pay: will there be major pay demands or likely pay strikes in the year ahead?

■ individual firms you expect trouble with

■ a specific campaign – either in connection with national union policy, or one you intend to launch locally (e.g., against racism, or to promote health and safety at work)

■ a new recruitment drive

■ problems caused by government policies

■ worries about closures and redundancies

■ any visits from national figures that you know of.

And of course you can **answer questions** put by the journalists. As always when bringing journalists to you, it is helpful to give them a story to go away with. This is not the main purpose of the briefing, but it will make it a more purposeful affair from the journalist's point of view if he/she can be sure there will be a story by the time the briefing is over.

If funds will run to it, **refreshment** should be provided.

This kind of annual briefing is not by any means restricted to big, regional union organisations. In a small town that has only a weekly newspaper, it can be done more informally. In medium-sized towns with a small evening paper, it could be done by the trades council, with the secretary introducing delegates from the main unions involved in that town's employment. Similarly, rank-and-file organisations or local pressure groups

(Shelter, Amnesty, CPAG, Community Health Councils) that have a specific campaign in mind for the coming year can organise a press conference (see Chapter 7); this can then be turned into a briefing meeting, so that the local journalists can meet face to face the people who will be leading the action.

Inviting journalists to give talks

One excellent way of making contact is to ask journalists to come and give talks about their work on a paper or at a broadcasting station. You can either write to an individual journalist or write to the editor, asking the editor to give the talk or nominate someone on his/her staff to do it.

Most editors are pleased to get such invitations, from any section of the community. You, in turn, will have an excellent chance to make personal contact in an unforced and natural manner – and, since the editor or journalist will be there to explain and justify editorial behaviour, it will be quite legitimate to present a challenging political argument in favour of better coverage of your point of view.

Making links with the NUJ

There are 180 branches of the National Union of Journalists in Britain. Thirty thousand working journalists are members. At their workplace (i.e., on a newspaper or in a broadcasting newsroom), the journalists are formed into **chapels**. Shop stewards are called 'father/mother' of the chapel.

Like all unions, the NUJ is mainly concerned with bread-and-butter economic issues – the pay and conditions of its members. It cannot act as a policeman for fair trade-union reporting throughout journalism. It does, however, have a *Code of Conduct*, so where there are serious complaints, trade-unionists should contact the Union (see Chapter 12). **But it is a good idea to forge trade-union links with the journalists' union even before things go wrong.**

> The author was a member of the Birmingham branch of the NUJ for some seven years, attending the branch meeting nearly every month. The period covered the Tory Industrial Relations Act, the great strikes by the miners of 1972 and 1974 (including the mass picketing of Birmingham's Saltley Coke depot) and the Labour victory of 1974 – all of which involved the active commitment of hundreds of thousands of West Midlands workers in trade-union and political struggle. Yet, during all that period, never once was the NUJ branch in Birmingham approached by another trade-union branch or group to form

some kind of link or to arrange a joint meeting to discuss one of the many trade-union issues of that period.

NUJ members have a double role: as **journalists** employed by businessmen to produce a product for profit, they report and comment on events and shape public opinion; but they are also **trade unionists,** with responsibilities as workers to colleagues in the trade-union movement. The conflict between these two roles is ever-present. Given the ideological framework of modern journalism, it is as unlikely that an appeal to journalists as trade unionists will result in their displaying pro-worker partiality in the product they manufacture as it is that an appeal to car-workers' solidarity would result in better-made cars.

Provided that this is understood, it is still worth trying to build contacts with the NUJ at branch and chapel level.

If you are involved in a trade-union struggle in a locality, write to the father or mother of the NUJ **chapel** at the local newspaper and ask if you can **send a speaker** to explain what your struggle is about to the next chapel meeting.

Make it clear that you are **not trying to demand or compel more favourable reporting** but want to talk as one trade unionist to others about the issues involved. Later on you can mention the newspaper coverage and make clear the objections that you may have. To ring or write and say, 'I'd like to come and tell the journalists why the coverage is so rotten', will guarantee a rebuff. The approach has to be, 'I'd be grateful if at the next chapel meeting you could give me a few minutes to explain why we are on strike and try and get a message of support from your chapel.'

Many chapels will be nervous of such an approach – but it should be tried, if only to confront NUJ members with their responsibilities (as workers) to others in struggle.

It should be easier to build contacts with a **branch.** Chapels are formed at the point of production, to bargain with employers; branches bring together NUJ activists from various chapels in a town or region.

Relationships with NUJ branches should be two-way. If you are involved in a particular struggle that is of interest to the whole trade-union movement in the area, you can write to the NUJ branch secretary to ask if you can make a short address to the next branch meeting. You can get the name and address of the appropriate branch secretary from the NUJ headquarters (Acorn House, 314–320 Grays Inn Road, London WC1 – 01-278-7916); or you can phone the local newspaper, ask for the newsroom, then asking for the Father or Mother of the NUJ chapel, and finally ask how to contact the NUJ branch secretary.

As with reporters and news editors, it is worth building up a personal relationship with the principal NUJ activists in chapels and branches. Some may be involved in local political or community activity and you can get to know them that way. They can also give advice on making contacts or issuing press releases as well as helping with NUJ contacts.

As well as offering to attend NUJ meetings, you can ask chapel and branch officers to come along to *your* meetings to talk about the work and structure of the NUJ in the locality.

There are many ways in which local trade unions and the NUJ can cooperate:

> During the NUJ's all-out provincial-newspaper journalists' strike (December 1978–January 1979) scores of NUJ chapels and thousands of provincial journalists took industrial action for the first time. They received impressive help by way of accommodation, cash and organisational advice from local trade unions.

N.B. There is also a body called the **Institute of Journalists.** It is not affiliated to the TUC (see page 44). **On no account should any trade unionist deal with/talk to/answer questions from a known IOJ journalist.** Quite apart from the old trade-union principle of not dealing with a non-unionised worker in an area where a TUC union organises, it is important to be aware that IOJ members tend to hold strong anti-union views. It is official NUJ policy to request unions not to deal with IOJ members. Several trades councils and union branches have passed formal resolutions refusing to deal with IOJ members in any way.

The NUJ's national policy is for all its branches to affiliate to a **trades council,** just as the NUJ is affiliated nationally to the TUC. However, the level of trade-union consciousness inside the NUJ is sometimes so low that branches do not know that they *can* (and *should*) join a trades council, let alone how to set about affiliating.

Trades Councils should ensure that the NUJ branch is affiliated. Officers should write to the local NUJ branch and ask it to join. Sometimes – particularly where older NUJ members predominate – the branch will be reluctant to do so; but the balance of political forces inside a branch can change from year to year, so, even if an NUJ branch rejects an approach to join one year, try again the following year and keep on asking the branch to join until it does.

What to say

Knowing how to react to press inquiries is something of an acquired skill. Journalists will want to talk to you to get information. The way they use that information is something over which you will have no control. Sometimes they will come briefed by the news editor to search for a particular angle. In other cases, the reporter will have been sent out cold and be expected to work out a story line from the facts as she/he sees them.

In a dispute, for example the journalist will tend to emphasise the following:

■ hardship to the public as consumers
■ hardship to other workers affected by the dispute
■ hardship to the management
■ damage to the company's ability to survive
■ conflict between workers
■ conflict between management and union
■ contrast between the importance of the improvement the workers seek and the damage it is causing.

To counter these attitudes, the following points could be stressed:

■ disruption to the public will be minimal
■ there need be no ill effect on other workers
■ management's offers are unreasonable, so rejection is justified
■ the dispute is management's fault
■ managements have the ability to pay (if a wage dispute)
■ wage levels are not as high as they appear to be
■ there's a distinction between the apparent grievance and the real one
■ an unofficial strike is not necessarily unjustified
■ industrial action was the democratic decision of the workers
■ workers have families to provide for – rent, mortgages, rates and bills to pay – and do not undertake industrial action lightly.

Many journalists go unbriefed to a story. The last thing they want is to be confronted with an excessively hostile or suspicious spokesman. This can lead to antipathy and resentment, which is counter-productive.

Be frank with a journalist when the story is one which traditionally involves a hostile media approach.

Interviewed on ITN about his members' decision not to provide emergency cover during the one-day public-service workers' strike in January 1979, the COHSE convenor of London ambulancemen said to the reporter: 'You people are always accusing us. Why don't you put the same question to David Ennals (the Secretary of State for Health) when he closes down a kidney unit at Hammersmith which was saving hundreds of lives?'

If the journalist – whether on the phone or at a news conference – displays an obvious prejudice in favour of a particular story line, turn the tables and ask what he or she thinks the story is all about. Then **point out alternative emphases.**

At a news conference called on behalf of Right to Work marchers at the TUC Congress in 1976, BBC reporter Vincent Hanna asked the Right to Work organising secretary, John Deason, if he was genuinely unable to find work or if he had simply decided to work full-time for the Right to Work campaign. Deason – a noted Socialist Workers' Party militant, who was blacklisted in the engineering industry – said to Hanna: 'Vincent, if you can find a single engineering employer to give me a job . . .' The rest was drowned in laughter.

Points to remember when contacted by a journalist

■ **Telephones aren't people.** About three-quarters of the journalist's fact-and-opinion gathering is done on the telephone. It is an important tool in the business, and journalists are good at using it. People tend to be more garrulous on the telephone than face-to-face. This suits the journalist, who will keep you talking until he/she has the information he/she wants. A good way of disciplining yourself is to **pretend that the journalist who is talking to you on the telephone is in fact interviewing you in front of your colleagues: say nothing on the phone that they would complain about if you said it in front of them.**

Telephones cannot convey the subtle language of face movements, which are a crucial part of communication. If possible, therefore, you should ask the journalist to meet you personally (the telephone keeps a distance between the journalist and the 'victim'; it is more difficult – though not impossible – to write cruelly about someone you have met in the flesh). Nine times out of ten, however, the journalist will not be able to meet you personally, because of his production schedule.

Never refuse to talk just because it is on the telephone. That will make journalists hostile, and suspicious that you are hiding something. Talk on the telephone, but **take care.**

■ **Are you the right person to comment?** If you feel that

you are not the person to be quoted on a particular subject, **then say so.** Tell the reporter how to contact the right person.

There is an understandable temptation to offer your own thoughts for publication because they are good ones and you may like seeing your name in print. But, if negotiations are currently taking place, **the wrong statement from the wrong person can cause havoc.** If the dispute (or the stance your union has taken) is a controversial one, journalists may be on the look-out for any split in the union ranks: a casual throwaway remark suggesting lack of support can be transformed through aggressive newspaper treatment into headlines and stories implying massive disaffection inside the membership.

Some branches or unions take formal decisions on who can and cannot speak to the press. It certainly makes sense to channel press communications through one person who is accountable to the membership (see Chapter 13, on **press officers**), and journalists will appreciate having a central point of contact with someone who can speak officially and authoritatively on behalf of colleagues or the organisation generally. On the other hand, there can be occasions when that individual is not available and reporters are desperate to get a comment. In this case, if you are in a position to comment, do so – but in fairly general terms. If journalists put you under pressure to comment because they cannot get hold of anyone else, insist that you are described as 'a spokesperson' and avoid getting your name in the papers.

■ **If you have nothing to say, say so.** Do not waste journalists' time, and don't let them waste yours. If you don't want to make a statement, say so straightaway. **Explain why.** Tell the reporter either that you cannot comment because you are not the right person (and tell him or her how to contact someone who *can* speak), or that the situation is very difficult/delicate and you don't want to say anything at the moment. It is helpful if you can tell the journalist when you *will* be making a statement. It is important to give some explanation as to why you are saying nothing; if you do not, suspicions will be aroused.

■ **Don't hurry: think/slow down/call back.** There is absolutely no need to provide an immediate response to a journalists' request for information or comment. If you are called upon to comment upon a situation you know and have views about then, obviously, go ahead and give an answer. But if the query relates to something you are not completely familiar with, or – which is more likely – to an issue or an event about which you have not thought very deeply, then do not rush in with a statement. Ask the *journalist* about the situation, while you gather your thoughts. Better still, ask if you can call back in five or ten minutes so that you can work out an exact answer or find out more information. Make sure you do call back. The journalist will feel let down if you don't and will only telephone again in a more irritated mood. Few journalists phone up with such a tight deadline that they cannot wait five minutes. In that time you can ensure that your response reflects what you really want to say, instead of it being a half-thought-out reaction which will annoy both you and your colleagues when you see it in the paper.

■ **Write it down – and stuff it with facts.** Comment and statements ('quotes', in journalistic jargon) can look very different in cold print compared with what you think you are saying to a reporter. If you want to see what it could look like, you should write down the main points you want to make and construct a juicy, hard-hitting statement of opinion that will catch the eye when read. True, many people hit upon the most dramatic way of making a point unrehearsed as they speak, and there is no doubt that some of the most pungent points made to reporters are remembered precisely because of their spontaneity; but it is generally difficult, especially on the telephone, to come up with the exact phrase, and it is helpful to have jotted down some key points beforehand.

Above all, the discipline of writing down what you want to get over to the media will force a concentration on facts. Hard facts are what news is made of: if you are to get a reporter to tell your side of the story fairly, you must provide solid, ascertainable facts to back your case. This is particularly important when the reporter arrives with a preconceived story line. She/he will not be interested if you say that it is wrong and unfair. His or her mind will be changed only by factual evidence.

Writing down your main points also ensures that you have them all covered when you talk to the reporter. In conversation, with the reporter controlling the questions, it is easy to forget to make one or two points that are crucial to your case. If you have them written down, you can always bring them into the interview (even if the reporter does not ask directly about them) by saying, 'Look, there's a couple of other important points in this story that you ought to know about' – and away you go!

■ **Phone again if you have more to say.** It sounds obvious, but many people think that once the interview with the reporter is over no further communication is possible. If you have new information, or if you forgot to make an important point, you should get hold of the reporter at once. The reporter won't mind, especially if the new point makes the story a better one. If you are being interviewed, you should always ask for a phone-number where you can contact the reporter. If the reporter isn't in when you call the newsroom, ask for a message to be left.

If necessary, call back two or three times. Don't worry about pestering reporters, provided that (1) you genuinely have extra or new information, and (2) you don't waste time with general chatter or going over ground already covered in previous communications.

■ **'Off the record' 'unattributable' 'don't say I told you, but . . .'.** Just because newsmen and women and their sources sometimes have a common interest in seeing details of an event published, there is no automatic need for the latters' name to be published. If you do not want your name used but are willing to give the reporter the information she/he wants, you must say right away that what you are saying is 'unattributable' and that she/he must not use your name. Alternatively, say that your comment is 'off the record' – which is usually taken to mean that what you say is to help and guide the reporter but should not be written up. Reporters are perfectly used to these terms: senior politicians, trade-union leaders and company PROs often try and manipulate news by giving extensive unattributable and off-the-record briefings which are aimed at getting over a particular story line without accepting personal responsibility. Whenever you see the phrase, 'I understand that . . .' it means that the reporter has been told something on an unattributable basis.

It is vital that you establish whether or not you can be quoted directly **as soon as the reporter contacts you.** If you don't, the reporter will assume that anything you say can be written down and reproduced in part or wholly in the story she/he subsequently writes. Most reporters take a good shorthand note of what you say; unless you tape-record the whole conversation, it will be little use complaining afterwards of inaccurate quoting. The reporter's note is there, and managements back their journalists. Nor does the moan, 'I didn't know I was going to be quoted', impress journalists. You must tell them *at the outset* if the interview is 'unattributable' or 'off the record'. **You can't do it retrospectively** – or at least, you can *try* and say half-way through that the last bit has been off the record; but, to a journalist who is not likely to need your cooperation again, your off-the-record demand will be disregarded for the portion of the interview that has gone by.

What you *can* do is have a mixed interview, by stating in advance of a particular piece of information that it is off the record – 'Look, this next bit is strictly off the record, but we reckon the managing director wants to sell off the factory cheap because he needs to raise cash in a hurry. You might look into his life-style and social acquaintances."

Local reporters, who may have to come back to you over a period for quotes and information, will in general treat off-the-record confidences scrupulously. National newspaper reporters in pursuit of a one-off story can be more careless (as they say on Fleet Street, 'Move in, move on, move out'!). It is better therefore, if you don't know the reporter, to tell only what you would be willing to see published next to your name.

Where you are confident about your relationship with the journalist, you need not fear that your name will be revealed. Journalists are proud about keeping their sources confidential, and some have resisted pressure from managements and others to reveal them even to the extent of going to prison (as did two Fleet Street journalists in 1962) rather than provide names.

Don't overdo demands that something be treated as off the record. Use it when you feel strongly that you cannot be mentioned; but remember that, unless you are providing information of high, obvious news value, reporters will suspect what you tell them.

■ **How 'yes' becomes a sentence.** One of the oldest tricks in the reporter's trade is to put a long question to you and then, when you say 'yes' in agreement, deem you to have made the statement implied in the question.

For example:

Reporter: 'Wouldn't you say, Mr Smith, that some members of the divisional council are likely to be very worried and concerned about the girls at Blackings walking out on the say-so of the branch secretary without getting official blessing first? Wouldn't you think that a bit irresponsible?'
Smith: 'Yes, I suppose it is really.'
This exchange, if written up, can appear as:

An internal row broke out today inside the General Clerical Union following a wildcat stoppage of telephonists at Blackings.
The GCU's Regional Secretary, Mr Tom Smith, condemned the unofficial walkout as irresponsible, and said

the GCU divisional council was very concerned about the action of the branch secretary involved, Ms Joan Brown.

'I am very worried about the women at Blackings walking out on the say-so of their branch secretary, without getting official blessing first from the divisional council or myself,' Mr Smith said.

There is nothing intrinsically dishonest or unethical about this technique. After all, journalists are professionally trained to turn out succinct and punchy prose. If they succeed in summing up a point rather effectively, even the most verbose politician may well bow to their superior ability and say, 'Yes, you can quote me as saying that.' However, it is a device used more often to trap the unwary than to sharpen style.

If you get asked a long rambling question which implies the answer 'yes', say a firm 'NO' and go on to say 'What I *would* say is . . .' You can joke with reporters and tell them that it's no use trying to put words into your mouth: 'I have only got one thing to say on this, and that is . . .' Watch out for key words in the question, such as 'condemn', or 'irresponsible', or 'victimisation' – they will seem much stronger when coming as a direct quote from you.

Beating around the bush. It is surprising how long you can spend talking to a reporter and how little will appear as written copy. If you tape-recorded the conversation it would seem repetitious and circular, with the same ground being covered many times. This is another common reporter's technique: to keep coming back to a subject, each time from a slightly different angle, in the hope that you will provide a give-away sentence which gives the reporter either the information she/he is looking for or a quote to make the story more exciting. Again, it is not a dishonest technique. In fact, it is rather like a negotiation session: each side bargains to get something from the other, but they approach the goal by different routes in the hope that as one question (or negotiator's argument) fails another will unlock the answer (or the boss's coffers).

The object of this exercise, from the reporter's point of view, is to get on good terms with you by means of a rambling, fairly general conversation and then, having lulled you into a sense of false security, to plant a question which will get an unguarded reply. Also, as the circular conversation goes on, you may lose the thread of the points you wanted to make and fail to emphasise your case sufficiently.

This technique can work both ways, because the repeating of questions by the reporter can give you a chance to make a point *more* dramatically the second time round. However, if you feel that you have already said as much as you want to say and given all the information you are prepared to make available, then it is worth cutting short a rambling conversation. Just say, politely but firmly, to the reporter: 'I'm sorry, I think we've covered all the ground and there's honestly nothing more that I can say. In any case, I've got to dash for a meeting, I'm late for it anyway.' The latter sentence is one worth using any time you want to get rid of a reporter. Simply cutting short an interview or a meeting with a reporter can cause friction. Giving a reasonable excuse, even if it is a white lie, about why the conversation must end is more acceptable.

■ **Be careful about simple denials.** If a reporter contacts you with some information – an accusation, say, or a statement from management or from trouble-making elements inside the union – which you know is utterly wrong, it may be that your flat denial will turn it into a publishable story. Newspapers do not like beginning any story negatively, but *watch out* – **sometimes it is precisely the denial that allows the story to be used at all:**

Trade-union officials strongly denied last night accusations that the union had arranged a deal with Brown's Ltd for the closure of the local bearings factory leading to 800 redundancies.

'There is no truth whatsoever in the charge,' said Harry Weeks, district official for the General Engineers Union.

If you are contacted with utterly wrong information, it is not a bad precaution to insist on going off the record before you say anything, so that you can make up your mind whether or not a denial from you in the paper would be advantageous. If not, say that you cannot be quoted but that you can assure the reporter that to your knowledge the facts are completely wrong. Say something like: 'I'm sorry, there's nothing in it – and if you run the story the paper will look a bit silly.' The reporter may threaten to print a statement that goes, 'When contacted, Harry Weeks declined to comment.' There is nothing you can do about that, but it may be a price worth paying for not allowing your name to be used negatively to prop up a harmful story.

9.

Dealing with television

Television journalists / technical staff /
electronic news-gathering and video tape
recording / how television is made / television
interviews / getting cash from television

Television journalists

When it comes to newspapers, you are likely to deal only
with reporters. Television is more complicated. There are several
different types of journalistic function in operation, and these
need to be distinguished if you are to judge how much authority
each possesses.

Researchers

The researcher is at the bottom of the television journalists' pyramid. He or (very often) she has different functions
according to the programmes worked for. For a 6 p.m. regional
television magazine programme or ITN's *News at One*, for example, the researcher may well double up as one of the newsroom
scriptwriters (see below).

The routine programme researcher will contact you to find
out the basic 'Ws' (Who, What, Where, When, Why) of the
story. She/he will also ask about the possibility of filming and, if
the producer wants a studio interview, whether you or a colleague can come to the studio at the required time. A researcher
on a major television current-affairs programme, on the other
hand, has a different role. She/he can be doing the work of a
serious investigative journalist or, as in the case of some heavy-
weight current-affairs output (*Weekend World, Panorama*), what
virtually amounts to academic research.

There are two things you must never forget about researchers:

■ **they can always be over-ruled.** No researcher should

ever make a definite promise, such as 'You'll be interviewed by yourself for three minutes' or 'I'm sure we'll show film of the unsafe machinery'. In fact, a good researcher should always make clear that the dictates of television production and the desires of the producer or editor make the offering of guarantees impossible. The researcher's word is never final.

■ **the researcher's loyalty is to his or her programme, to the boss and, at the end of the day, to the company which pays the salary.** No matter how strong the researcher's commitment to the story (or to the issue or individuals covered in the story), he or she will have to accept orders or face the consequences of resignation or dismissal.

Reporters

It may be the producers and the editors who control the programmes (see below), but the names known to the public are those of the reporters and correspondents. News reporters will often have complete control over the reports they produce – doing the linking commentary, cutting the interview into segments, deciding which backing film will be used. Current-affairs reporters – those on programmes like *Panorama* and *TV Eye* – work very closely with the producer on both the script and the manner in which the report is put together. Sometimes a news reporter will have to send the interview, commentary and film back to the newsroom, where it will be assembled by a script-writer or sub-editor (see below).

Like their colleagues in newspapers and radio, television reporters have widely differing levels of knowledge and experience about workers' problems and trade-union issues. **Full-time industrial correspondents** on national television have tremendous knowledge but **tend to look at things from the point of view of the union headquarters and the senior full-time officials** with whom they have most contact.

A newly recruited reporter from one of the smaller regional-television newsrooms may find him/herself out on a story about a strike and be uncertain about the wider issues involved and unsure about which person – full-time official or picketing shop steward – is the most appropriate interviewee. **Some of the worst television coverage of industrial affairs comes from ignorance rather than malice.**

Scriptwriters and sub-editors

Only about half of the average television-news bulletin

consists of reporters' items or studio interviews. The rest is made up of news items read out by the newsreader, or edited stretches of film with the newsreader reading the story while the film is running. The words in the news items, whether read direct by the newsreader or spoken over film, are written by journalists working in the television newsroom. These are called 'sub-editors' (or 'news assistants') in the BBC, and 'scriptwriters' at ITN and in most ITV companies.

Just as for newspaper sub-editors, their job is to take copy from national news agencies, freelance news agencies, press releases and other sources of news information and write news stories suitable for broadcasting. The television scriptwriter will also be given unedited newsfilm and told to produce a film story – i.e., a news story linked to what the film shows. She/he will work with a film editor (see below), who will cut the film to the scriptwriter's instructions. The scriptwriter will be told to produce a story of a specific length – 'Give me forty seconds on the sit-in, followed by twenty-five seconds on the dustman's stoppage', the news editor will say.

Television scriptwriters have very little time in which to tell their stories. Newsreaders speak at the rate of three words a second, so even a ten-minute news bulletin in which the newsreader spoke non-stop (in fact there are lots of pauses when film is shown, and little gaps when words are not being spoken) would consist of only 1,800 words. That amounts to about two and a half columns in a newspaper.

Television scriptwriters tend to work from written material given to them. In the course of a day's work they do not have much contact, journalistically speaking, with the outside world. If they receive freelance or PA copy about an event, they will rely on it to provide the basis of what they write for the story that is transmitted. **It is therefore important that they have available your side of the story in the form of a press release or statement.**

Directors/producers

The titles of 'director' and 'producer' are imprecise. The job done by the journalist bearing either of these titles varies from programme to programme and from company to company.

You may meet someone who says that he or she is the director (more common in ITV) or the producer (BBC usage) of a particular programme or piece of film, and that he wants your help or involvement. This person will probably either be producing a longish item for a programme like *Nationwide* or one of the regional programmes, or be making a long film – say 15 minutes or more – for one of the major current-affairs programmes, such as *Panorama* or LWT's *London Programme*. She/he will have overall responsibility for organising the research for the item, for briefing the reporter (and, in many cases, writing the script), for telling the cameraman what to film, and for the editing of the film and its final preparation for transmission.

Clearly it is important that the director/producer of a long film has maximum access to the facts and analysis from your point of view. You should ask for a meeting to discuss what kind of film she/he hopes to make. After the filming is over, keep in touch. Often there is a gap between the shooting of the film and the final editing. If there are any new developments – even minor ones – that will help your case, contact the director/producer and pass on the information.

Editors/producers/news editors

The BBC and the big television companies are riddled with top-management bureaucrats in their news and current affairs departments. The NUJ once calculated that there were more than one hundred senior BBC employees who had titles connected with editorial/executive responsibility yet who, after careful examination, could not be said to fulfil any useful journalistic function.

There are some senior journalists, however, who do take 99 per cent of the final decisions on news bulletins, feature magazines and current-affairs programmes. Their titles, again, vary from department to department and between the BBC and ITV. The man in charge of *ATV Today* from Birmingham is called the Executive Producer. His opposite number in charge of Birmingham BBC's *Midlands Today* has the title of Midlands News Editor. The person in charge of *Weekend World* is called the Editor, as is the man who is in charge of *Panorama*. Their equivalent who runs *World In Action* is called the Executive Producer.

This galaxy of titles is only important in so far as it is necessary to identify clearly the person in charge of a programme. On a daily programme, she/he will decide in the morning what stories to cover and what the story line should be. The researcher will report to him/her and the reporters will show him/her their filmed reports before transmission. He/she will also make the final decision on who comes into the studio for interview and which items get dropped from the running order because of time pressure.

Technical staff

Alongside the television journalists at all levels are the workers responsible for turning their 'creative' desires into transmittable television. Television is an elitist business; the unions have not paid enough attention to the role of these technical workers, or encouraged them to ask for a greater share of editorial control. As it is, they can play an important part in shaping the message that goes out to the viewer.

Cameramen

Cameramen (there is resistance here too to the idea of employing women) operate under instructions from a director, **but they are the only people whose eyes actually see what is being recorded.** If a film cameraman shoots an interview sequence so that the employer's face is always in full, perspiring close-up while the union spokesman is shot sitting comfortably and authoritatively behind a desk then, irrespective of what is said, the image created will be favourable towards the union. (Usually it is the other way round!)

Electricians

Electricians responsible for setting up studio lights or providing the lighting for interior sequences can also subtly alter the way an interviewee looks.

Film editors

Film editors cut the film to the length that is actually transmitted. For every second of film you see on television, up to ten seconds will have been discarded on the film editor's floor.

> Newsfilm coverage of the Grunwick mass picketing often showed the police struggling against a mass of shoving picketers. The film of a Special Patrol Group policeman hitting people full in the face without any provocation was never shown. That ended up in the big black plastic bags into which film editors dump their discarded film.

Most film editing is done under the supervision of a journalist (producer, reporter or scriptwriter), and it is he/she who takes the responsibility for what gets broadcast. But film editors often get asked to do the preliminary cutting of a sequence, and when the journalists are inexperienced or unconfident they will take advice from a film editor on how to cut some film. In both cases, **the film editor can be crucial in deciding which visual images are actually shown.**

Electronic news-gathering and videotape recording

In the United States, Japan and West Germany, television newsrooms are increasingly using videotape rather than film to record news events and interviews. Videotape (VTR) records pictures directly on to tape and can be edited immediately – unlike film, which has to be chemically processed (i.e., developed and printed). VTR equipment can be carried by one person and it is now technically possible for the whole operation of recording pictures and sound and speaking a commentary to be done by one person – the reporter.

Also being developed are lightweight outside-broadcast cameras for news coverage. These would mean that a camera-person could transmit live pictures back to a studio while walking alongside a demonstration.

Both developments are being carefully watched by the broadcasting unions because of the serious implications for staffing levels.

How television is made

Like the news in newspapers, television news is a skilfully manufactured product. The same kinds of journalist, and similar journalistic values, operate in both. **The press releases you send to a newspaper office will do for the television newsroom (and for radio newsrooms too).**

Television, though, is hampered by the way it is produced. A newspaper journalist can extract an interview from you on the telephone while you are having a bath, and it can make a sensational front-page story. For television, either you have to go to them or the film crew has to come to you. That means dovetailing times and places. For the shop steward from Whitehaven who is asked to appear on BBC *Look North*, which comes from Newcastle, it means the best part of an eight-hour shift by the time he/she has got to Newcastle, taken part in the programme and returned to Whitehaven. It is a lot of effort for three minutes on television. But that three minutes may be seen by a couple of

1. A fully-crewed film unit used in major documentaries:
   left to right: reporter, production assistant, driver, sound
   recordist, lighting technician, camera operator, director,
   researcher, assistant sound recordist, assistant camera operator

2. A regional television news feature film crew:
   left to right: reporter, sound recordist, director, camera operator
   (national news film crews would normally dispense with the
   director)
3. A two-person video-recording crew:
   camera operator and reporter (the camera incorporates a uni-
   directional microphone and the entire unit is portable)

million people, including workmates, the management or proprietor, other trade unionists, local politicians and other journalists – a far bigger, if more diffused, audience than can ever be got from personal meetings.

In March 1979, the organisation Campaign Against Racism in the Media (CARM) made a 30-minute access programme in the BBC *Open Door* series. CARM was denied news film by both the BBC and ITN, but made a powerful attack on the racial stereotyping in television current-affairs coverage and comedy programmes. The programme – called 'It ain't half racist, mum' – took months to plan. CARM organised a preview screening, and the next day the programme was the lead item in all the national-newspaper television columns. The *Daily Mail* said: 'It was a strong programme saying what has long needed saying.'

Future planning

More than any other medium, television relies on future planning. Television news boasts that it *'brings you news as it happens'*, or that television newsfilm shows *'what actually took place'* – unlike newspaper reports, which can only convey a second-hand impression. This ignores both the editorial decision that led to the cameras being there in the first place, to cover the event and so guarantee that it is made into a piece of 'news', and the costly organisational effort involved in getting skilled technicians and their expensive, complicated equipment to the right place at the right time.

Even for those stories which are *certain* to be covered – any national strike involving a service industry, for example – the television newsroom plans in advance. In a very good book which describes how BBC and TV Radio news is made (*Putting 'reality' together: BBC news*, Dr Philip Schlesinger, Constable 1978), the author gives this account of future planning in the national BBC TV Newsroom:

Every Thursday, at Television News, a Home News Futures meeting is held, which is attended by the Editor and Deputy Editor of Television News, the Home News Editor and his deputy, the five assistant editors who take it in turn to act as editor of the day, and the news organiser (planning). The agenda on this occasion is compiled by News Intake, and is called the Weekly Futures List.

The Home News Editor runs through the futures list for the next seven days and tries to 'sell' the stories to the output editors. Discussion at the meeting is a mixture of news judgement and logistical talk. The list contains details of advanced arrangements made with the BBC's regional newsrooms for sending pictures over video circuits for recording in London. Indeed, as in all television news discussions, the 'picture merit' of proposed stories is a highly salient factor.

Similar meetings are held every week in every television newsroom or current-affairs production office. An internal conference with a much shorter time perspective is held every morning in each newsroom or office where there is a daily programme. It too discusses the news prospects and logistical problems involved in covering the day's news.

If you want your story to be covered, it is vital that the television producers know about it in advance. Certain other factors need to be remembered about organising stories with an eye to television coverage.

■ **Television film needs light.** Film cameras can only shoot what they see, and if the light is fading they cannot see much. This is changing with new developments in fast-film technology, but in winter very little film is shot of external scenes from about the middle of the afternoon onwards.

■ **Film (or videotape) has to get back to the studio in good time.** Film has to be transported physically to the studio before it can be shown. Once there, it has to be developed and printed before it can be edited, let alone transmitted. All this takes time. For stories happening on the fringe of a coverage area – Peterborough, say, which is served by television stations in Birmingham or Norwich and is a good two hours' drive on poor roads from either – the producer will need to know that he/she will get a *very* good film report in return for sending a crew and a reporter all that way when, in the same period, they could provide two separate stories from areas closer to base.

Television interviews

This section is divided into five parts:
■ before the interview
■ general rules about being interviewed
■ film interviews
■ studio interviews
■ remote studio interviews.

It does not really matter whether you are having a half-hour face-to-face with Robin Day or (which is more likely), two minutes on a regional-television magazine – the business of being interviewed on television always requires careful preparation and even more careful execution. It comes a lot easier with practice of course, but only a tiny handful of people get to appear regularly on television. On those rare occasions when you are invited to appear, **you should be in a position to do the best by your case, your workmates, your members, and yourself.**

Big firms, government departments and public corporations have long recognised this. Some of them rely on 'spokesmen' to represent the company, but more and more companies are training their senior executives in the art of appearing on television. They are sent away on £500-a-week courses run as a sideline by some of the big names in television newscasting.

Trade unionists, whether general secretaries or shop stewards, are adept at communicating. But the traditional techniques of trade-union communication – ranging from the blockbusting speech at the TUC to a divisional organiser writing to his branches explaining how a regional reorganisation is to be implemented; from picket-line speeches to a shop steward telling his members how a complex new bonus scheme will operate – all these techniques need to be forgotten when it comes to appearing successfully on television both on film and in the studio.

Before the interview

Before you start to work out the right approach and techniques for being interviewed, you have to ask several practical questions:

■ what is the purpose of the interview?

■ does the reporter or producer simply want to extract information?

■ will you be confronted by other people – management, or fellow trade unionists – who disagree with you?

■ will the interview be live or recorded?

■ who is the interviewer going to be?

■ is the interview for local or national output?

■ what kind of programme is the interview to be used in?

■ will it be transmitted straight, or cut into little pieces and woven into a sequence?

■ when will the interview be broadcast? (remember that television film makers can work months in advance)

■ who else is being interviewed, and in what sequence will the interviews be shown?

■ if invited to a studio, will you get equal billing and chance with the other guests?

■ what is the general line of questioning going to be?

In a neat phrase coined by Peter Jay and a former colleague from LWT's *Weekend World* programme, John Birt, much of television journalism suffers from 'a bias against understanding'. Their argument is that television journalism is good – sometimes very good – at telling the straightforward 'what, who, when and where' but is poor at explaining the 'why' and the 'how' of a situation. This is crucial in industrial reporting, when a simple narrative of events can mask the underlying reasons for a dispute or policy development.

By only providing a selection of 'facts' and avoiding any personal bias, **a reporter can actually seriously mislead his/her viewers if he/she does not also offer an interpretation of 'why' an event is happening.** Another problem is the television journalist's need for pictures. Thirty seconds of scuffling with the police on a picket line will easily command a place in a television-news bulletin; but it may be difficult to explain in equally compelling film terms the reasons behind the strike, so they tend to get forgotten.

None of this should put you off being interviewed, but do bear it in mind. Without being malicious or wishing deliberately to distort, a reporter or producer is looking for **'good television'**, **which might not coincide with the most effective presentation of your case.**

The other important questions to ask yourself concern your own approach to the interview:

■ **what** do you want to get out of it?

■ **to whom** are you going to address yourself? Are you aiming at your **members**? Do you want to convey a message to the **management** – perhaps one of determination, or a hint of compromise? Is it the **general public** you are trying to convince? Do you want to gain more active support from **other trade unionists** in the area?

In the average three-minute interview or discussion on a regional 6.00 p.m. programme – let alone the forty seconds of a national news bulletin – you have to have narrowed down the points you want to make and worked out how to make them as effectively as possible.

Decide on the **three main points** you want to get over. For example:

- low wages
- the company's profits
- the complete determination of your members.

Then decide on an effective way of making those points:

'The money these men/women get is so low they'd be better off on social security.'

'The average industrial wage is £100 a week. My members only get £42 a week. That's how badly paid they are.'

'On the money these people get most animals in the local zoo get better food and treatment.'

'This firm's profits have gone up by 30 per cent in the last year; they can easily afford our claim.'

'This company made £1·3 million profit last year. That's £7,500 profit per employee. All we want is a fair share.'

'Look, the managing director is on £27,000 a year. The executives take home £12,000 a year. My members are lucky if they get £60 a week. There's enough profit for everyone to have a living wage.'

'They'll still be on that picket line next Christmas unless they get a fair offer.'

'They're not being unreasonable. Go down and talk to them yourself. They're ordinary people who have been pushed around too long. They know in their hearts what a fair deal is and they'll stay out till they get one.'

'I've been involved in hundreds of disputes but I've never seen such determination. It could go on a long time and become very unpleasant if the management keep on refusing to have discussions.'

These are all the kind of remarks you might make about a dispute when chatting to a friend about it – describing it in an informal but human and forceful way. **Unprepared trade-unionists dropping nervously into jargon will only sound like bureaucratic speak-your-weight machines.**

Here is one trade-union regional official being interviewed after a meeting in a factory which is boiling over for an official strike:

'I'm sorry; all I'm prepared to say is that in connection with the problem I've had a full meeting with those that are involved as far as this situation is concerned and in regard to the context of the position I shall be making a full report to my executive.

'No I won't say anything else. I think I've made it all perfectly clear.'

The official was worried: firstly, he did not want to break the confidentiality of the factory meeting; secondly, he needed further authority before agreeing action. Fair enough. Just because you are on television you should not exceed your powers, nor should you ever get in the position of seeming to negotiate on television. But you can always talk generally about the mood and determination of the members and get in a side-swipe at the management. Or, if you want to cool things down, you can say: 'It's a very difficult problem and I don't think it would be helpful to either side, as we search for the correct solution, to start sounding off in public . . .'

It is a matter of deciding what you want to say and then sounding *human* when you say it.

Before we get into the detail of how to behave when the film or studio camera is actually staring at you, there are certain other points to remember before being interviewed.

■ Be modest. In the sense that just about all of us can open our mouths and talk, it can be said that broadcasting can be done by anybody. But some people are better than others. If a colleague, whether full-time or lay, is better than you on television (or radio) then push him or her forward. All television performing improves with experience but some people just happen to be more relaxed and effective performers on the box. On the other hand, don't be so consumed by humility that you refuse to appear when you *are* the right person or when you're the only person available.

■ Be available. Although a programme may not go out until 6.00 p.m., the schedule has to be planned as early as 11.00 a.m. Producers must know if you can come into a studio or if it is possible to record an interview.

■ If they leave a message to call, return it as soon as possible.

■ If you are locked in a meeting, send out a message to say when you will be free.

■ During a continuing dispute, make sure the television (and radio) newsrooms know when and where your daily news conference is. And don't hold it at 4.30 p.m. if you want to have your comments on film for that evening's local news.

■ Avoid the milling crowd of reporters after a factory or mass meeting. Identify the separate television film crews and tell them that there is no need to crowd because they will each get a separate interview. It only adds a few minutes, gives you more time to think and will enable you to come over more authoritatively. This is far better than the 'stag-at-bay' style of so many trade-union interviews, when the trade unionist is shoved against a wall while reporters jostle with their questions.

■ **Be neat.** Television is about images. Viewers will quickly forget who you are or what you've said; but if you look pleasant and are neatly dressed, you are already part way to getting their sympathy. You don't have to look like a tailor's dummy, but it seems foolish to alienate needlessly those viewers who may be put off by an unusual style of dress or appearance, however acceptable it is at your workplace or amongst colleagues.

■ **Be careful where they film you.** A favourite television interview is outside the picket line or factory gate, with other workers milling round. This contrasts with the management interview, which shows the employers sitting calmly in their offices – the embodiment of continuous, responsible authority.

You can refuse to be interviewed surrounded by jostling, angry people. Either insist that the interview takes place a little later on when it is quieter, or suggest that you go back to an office or strike headquarters.

When you are filmed, be careful of the **background**. Most interviews are shot in medium close up – which means that your upper chest, shoulders and head are in view, together with any buildings, people or signs immediately behind you. In an office, arrange to have a suitable poster behind you on the wall. If you are being filmed outside a factory gate, get placards held up behind you as you are being filmed. If the television journalists arrange to film you at home or at the office, try to make sure there are some bookshelves behind you. Studies in the United States have shown that, where there are books in the background, the interviewee comes over as sensible, respected and authoritative.

Sometimes, of course, you will want the film cameras to come down to the picket line to see the determination of those on strike; or you may want to get a camera into a factory or hospital to film unsafe or dirty working conditions. In that case, talk to the researcher, reporter or producer and explain that you think they will be able to get good pictures if they come and do the interview at that particular place.

■ **Be sure to ask to see how you will be introduced.** This only applies in live studio interviews. Ask to see the presenter's script (dozens are duplicated before the programme starts, and there is always a spare one lying around), and see how your item is being introduced. It will give you a good idea of how they will treat you in the interview.

For example, the presenter's script may read:

> CUE: 'There is growing concern about the dispute at Blackings, which has led to four thousand men being laid off in the motor industry. A local MP has denounced the thirty-eight screen inspectors at the centre of the dispute as being nothing better than industrial criminals, while the General Secretary of the union involved has appealed to the strikers to go back to work and not to put the jobs of other trade unionists in jeopardy. With me in the studio is the men's shop steward, John Smith.'

If he gets the chance to see that introduction, shop steward John Smith can kick up a fuss and try to get it changed so as to get some reflection of the workers' side into these opening remarks; or he can prepare himself to rebut sharply the implications in the introduction as soon as the interview begins. In any event, he can easily guess the general line the interviewer is likely to take.

■ **Be aware of who you are appearing with.** It sounds obvious, but too many trade unionists agree to come into the studio to take part in a discussion without finding out who their adversary will be. It is important to know, so that you can arm yourself with specific information about him or his company to use in argument. There is nothing sinister or improper about making the two sides in a dispute confront each other in the studio, but you need to know about it beforehand. It is quite likely that the television people will put you both into the same room – usually called the green room – **before you go into the studio.** Be friendly or be politely indifferent, as the mood takes you, but **do not get involved in an argument or give away any of the points you want to make.** Save that for when the millions are watching at home.

If the discussion involves a lot of people – as, say, in one of those television shows with a panel of 'experts' and others contributing from the general audience – be careful about where you are placed. One technique is to have four or five senior union and management people ranged either side of the presenter and then two or three short rows of seats for the workers. Those on the panel come over as more impressive and share the presenter's authority, while the group of workers may appear as an undisciplined rabble. **Don't play this game.** Decide amongst yourselves which two workers will represent your views, and insist that they be on the panel. Also, insist on a re-arrangement of the seating so that everyone is on an equal footing.

> When ATV made a programme about the Lucas Combine Shop Stewards' corporate plan, they invited a studio audience composed chiefly of trade-union members to put questions to the panel of experts. During the recording, however, it became clear that only the panel were expected to contribute. The lights were then dimmed and the audience were told the programme was over. Immediately, the Chairman of the Combined Shop Stewards' Committee stood up and said ATV were cheating them. The audience refused to leave the studio. They spoke to the camera-operators and technicians, who supported their right to participate. Under this pressure, the studio director agreed to re-record part of the programme and include questions and discussion from the audience.

■ **Find out the line of questioning in advance.** Most reporters or presenters will tell you roughly what they are going to ask, if only because it is embarrassing for them to have you dry up in the middle of an interview. If they forget to tell you, make sure you ask what questions will be put and what particular points the interviewer wants to get over. You may ignore some of his questions and get over some points you want to make that may not coincide with what he thinks is important, but you will do so with more confidence if you know what he is going to ask.

It can work both ways however. The interviewer can tell you:

> 'Well, I'll start off with the current situation in the dispute, then I'll put some criticisms that the strikers have gone a bit far on the picket line and then we can have one or two questions on where it all goes from here.'

But his actual first question can be a killer:

> 'Your own union won't recognise you, the local community have made clear they don't support the strike and, though they probably haven't told you, I gather that some of your

own members want a meeting to consider going back to work. What's your reaction?'

So, as well as finding out the general line, you should **try and get the interviewer to tell you the exact form of the first question** – because in most television interviews it is the first twenty seconds of the interview that set the tone for the remainder.

■ **Watch out for the killer questions.** Even where they have given a general advance notice of questions, many reporters will still slip in a very sharp, hard question that has not been previously mentioned. Be prepared for this. **You must be alert and ready for the unexpected at all times.**

■ **Make yourself at home.** If you are being interviewed at the studios, don't be put off because it's strange territory. Ask to be shown inside the studio where the interview is to take place, so as to get some feel of what it's like. If you want a cup of tea, or to make a phone call, or to be given some paper and a pen, just ask for it: they'll always oblige.

Some companies want you to be made up. There is no longer any technical need for this (there used to be in the days of less advanced cameras), but it is quite soothing to go away and be pampered for five minutes. It also ensures that you look your best. Despite appearances, television is the least natural thing on earth and electronic transmission can do odd things to what you normally look like. The make-up used is very light, normally a thin powder to stop your face shining under the lights.

Television studios are studded with lavatories and most people, either side of the camera, are nervous before a programme goes out. So don't worry about going to relieve yourself at any time up to your actual interview.

If you want a drink they will give you one and, in many cases, offer you as much as you want. **BE CAREFUL.** Some people say that a whisky can loosen your tongue before being interviewed. Others argue that even half a pint when combined with the hot lights and the increase in tension can make people come over as tipsy. Whatever your personal capacity, **one drink should be the maximum.**

Before the interview you are in a strong position. However badly you may think *you* need the *publicity*, **they need you too** (and most television interviews are still initiated from the inside). Whether they send a film crew out to interview you or ask you to come to the studio, a lot of time and money has already been spent and editorial decisions made on the assumption that you are willing to talk. So you can safely kick up a fuss to make sure the interview takes place in a context that is fair to you. **If you are unhappy, make a fuss. You are an essential ingredient.** They will go a long way towards accommodating an essential customer, however awkward.

During the interview

There are variations in technique according to:

■ whether you are being interviewed live or being recorded

■ whether on film or in the studio

■ whether one-to-one with the interviewer or in a general discussion

■ whether you are being interviewed where you are or from another studio (e.g., you are in Leeds and your questioner is in London).

But the basic rules hold good for any broadcast interview – television or radio.

■ **Know your facts.** You have to have all the relevant facts at your fingertips – the number of people involved, the number likely to be affected, the history of the dispute or policy development, facts about the opposition, statements made about the issue by other parties.

■ **Assume that you will be asked the question you would least like to answer** and work out how to answer it. Even if your head is stuffed full of facts and figures, pick carefully those you want to use to support your argument. A gushing waterfall of statistics only confuses viewers. Just because you know everything, you don't have to tell everything. Put over the facts confidently but not arrogantly. You may feel cocky in the studio, but you will come over in the home as an offensive know-all.

■ **Project yourself.** Although you are **having a conversation** with the interviewer and **not making a speech,** you should still deliberately inject more vitality and authority into your speaking than you would in a normal conversation. It is emphatically not a matter of trying to out-act Laurence Olivier but a matter of having that extra measure of controlled enthusiasm which will force the viewer at home to sit up. Paradoxically, you should both be relaxed but never relax – you should have that mixture of butterflies and relaxed concentration that a great batsman has when facing the world's fastest bowler. You should feel confident; but, if you don't feel a little tense, your interview will probably have little impact. Keep alert and mentally on your toes. This has to come over in more than your voice. Your face, and especially your eyes, should indicate that you find the questions interesting and challenging and that you are giving 100 per cent in answering them. Listen to the questions and look as if you are listening hard. **A dull, unresponsive face looks like a stale cod's head on television.**

■ **Make a good start.** The first answer is vital. Work out beforehand what you want to say in it. Ask the interviewer what his first question will be, not just in general terms but the precise words he will use. Try and fashion a response so that it both answers his question and gets over the important first point.

For example, you are involved in a strike which is under a great deal of pressure; but you know there is successful blacking being applied in other parts of the country. The reporter's introduction and first question may go something like this:

> *Reporter:* 'Now the strike at Browns. This morning, 63 out of the 150 strikers signed a petition asking to go back to work. They have also called for the resignation of their shop steward, Tom Smith. Well, he's with me here. Mr Smith, isn't this strike close to collapsing?'

Your first (gut) reaction may be to tackle all the implications in the question – to rebut the call for your resignation, to denounce the organisers of the petition. That would be fine, but utterly negative. It would mean that the reporter was de-limiting the area of discussion. Obviously you cannot ignore the question; nor, as it is the first question, can you use the old but still extremely useful technique of saying: 'I'll come back to that in a moment but what is really important . . .' Instead, you simply ignore all the implications and go on the offensive with the facts you want to put over in order to inject fresh heart into your flagging members. In response to the question posed – 'Isn't this strike close to collapsing?' – you reply:

> *Tom Smith:* 'No, not at all. In fact the very opposite. We've just had news today that about a dozen lorries with this firm's goods in them were turned away from warehouses in the North. Despite their brave face, this company is completely unable to move their goods. That's £20,000 in lost revenue this past two weeks. And it would cost less than a tenth of that to settle. Obviously our members are worried – it would be a very funny group of people who

enjoyed being on strike. But they all know – even my friends who have been going round with lists of illegible signatures realise – that this is one where we all have to stick together.'

If you can establish yourself with authority and vitality in the first twenty seconds (the answer above would take about 30 seconds to deliver), you have begun to dominate the interview.

■ **Look at the interviewer.** Always speak to the interviewer directly. Don't worry about where the camera or microphone are. Look him or her hard in the eyes, as if in a serious conversation. If you are in a studio, don't – even when you aren't speaking – look up or down and around the studio. One of the two or three cameras in use may be showing a wide-angle shot of you, or a 'reaction shot' of your face. If you aren't seen to be looking at the man asking the questions, you will look silly.

■ **Be serious but courteous.** It doesn't matter how much of a joker you may be in real life – **if you are representing other people on television you should go about it seriously.** And that means you should look and sound serious. You don't have to be pompous and compose your features like an undertaker's, but do avoid looking anxious to please. Do not smile unless something genuinely funny is said. Smiling for the sake of smiling will only make you look weak on the television set at home.

At the same time, however serious you are, you should treat the interviewer with courtesy. He is probably well known to the public. For many of the regular studio interviewers, particularly those in regional television, their relationship with people watching is almost that of a family friend; so, if you are curt or rude with the interviewer, you are insulting their friend. Conversely, if the interviewer is being rude to *you*, you will get the sympathy of the viewers. One ex-BBC-TV producer who now runs a school for teaching politicians how to appear on television has a rule that you can be rude to an interviewer only if he has been rude to you at least three times!

■ **Challenge the interviewer.** While remaining serious and courteous, you should **never let the interviewer get away with a question or statement that is untrue or grossly tendentious.**

Interrupt the interviewer, or wait until he or she has finished the question and say sharply, 'That's simply not true' or 'That's a completely unfair way of presenting the story' or 'The assumption in your question about extremists is nonsense. The people on strike are normal trade unionists, family men and women. The reason they democratically, without any pressure, decided to go on strike, is . . .', and so on.

One common interviewer's trick is to say, 'Some people say (or think) . . .', and then come out with a controversial opinion. It is a way of putting an opinionated point of view to the interviewee while the interviewer retains an air of apparent neutrality. Challenge that by tackling him directly: 'I've not heard anyone say that' or 'you've obviously been talking to the management, but ordinary people think the opposite . . .'

On the other hand, **if the interviewer** (by question or statement) **says something that you agree with, then feel free to say so:** 'Yes, I completely agree with you' or 'You're absolutely right, but what is just as important is . . .' The latter technique allows you to deflect a question in order to bring in something you have not so far been able to get over.

There are all sorts of deflecting phrases you can use: 'That's a very fair point/question, but one thing we've all forgotten is . . .' or 'Before I answer that question in detail I want to make it clear that . . .' or 'I don't think that's the main issue; what it's really all about is . . .' Watch seasoned television performers, senior politicians or trade-union leaders, and you'll see several methods that can be used to deflect a direct question and put over the point that you want to make.

■ **Above all, keep it short.** As in all communication, the briefer you can be the better. Long rambling sentences are killers – whether on television, on the radio or in the press. The audience haven't got your detailed knowledge, nor do they share your keen interest. They want the facts and arguments made short and sharp. Keep them that way.

Film interviews

Film interviews get cut to pieces in the editing room in lots of different ways and for different reasons. In daily news, time is often the biggest pair of scissors. A two-minute film interview done at noon may command only 30 seconds on the *News at 5.45* if 'better' news broke during the afternoon. In national news bulletins – the *Nine O'Clock News* or *News at Ten* – interviews very rarely last longer than one and a half minutes, if that. Even though only 60 or 90 seconds appears on the screen, the interview will have lasted longer – possibly four or five minutes.

Remember that you are being recorded on film, and that what has been recorded once can be recorded again. If you feel you are making a complete mess of an answer, just come to a stop and **ask if you can do it again.** A trick to make this appear less contrived is to have a major coughing fit, or suddenly swear and then stop in embarrassment. They will have to start again. If, at the end of the interview, you feel you have not made out your case or you have missed an important point – ask if you can do it again.

Television journalists want to have the best interviews possible. In the eyes of their colleagues and superiors there is no credit in bringing back an interview with someone who is stumbling and nervous, or dull and longwinded. If anything the opposite is true. The television journalist prides him or herself on getting people to give 'good' interviews ('good' in the sense of being impressive to watch, although not necessarily 'good' in the most effective presentation of your case).

Sometimes it is worth making a deal with the producer or reporter – an agreement to say just what will be broadcast and not have any superfluous questions and answers to be lost in the cutting room. The television journalist may have already worked out the shape of his or her story and will say, 'I think I want to bring out three main points from the trade-union side and I'd like you to put them over quickly and with as much punch as possible.' It may seem as if s/he is dictating to you; but, provided that you decide what will be said in that short space of time, at least you will have got the almost certain guarantee that it will be broadcast.

It is helpful when being filmed to have a friend or colleague there, to listen to what you are saying. Firstly, you can be told if you have left out an important point, so that you can ask to do the interview (or part of it) over again. Secondly, there is a witness (who should take notes) to what was said, questions and answers, in the interview. If what appears on screen is a travesty of the interview, you have a **witness** to that effect and your complaint will not rely solely on your memory. (The problem of complaints about television is covered in Chapter 12.)

Watch out during establishing shots and cutaways. Before the reporter asks a single question, the film crew will want to shoot some film which shows the two of you together. These 'establishing shots' are used to help the editing of the film so that the reporter can go smoothly from identifying who you are in the commentary – i.e., 'I then spoke to Sue Brown, leader of the tenants' committee' (the picture shows reporter and Ms Brown together) – to his first question – 'and asked her why they were occupying the office' (the picture then cuts to Ms Brown's face answering the question).

When doing the establishing shots (which normally take seconds at the start of the interview), just look normally at the reporter. Do not grin or move your face about.

After the interview is over, the reporter will have to repeat some of the questions directly into the camera. This is necessary because, during the interview, the camera will have been filming your face; if, when the film is transmitted, the viewer is to see the reporter asking a question the reporter has to repeat that question directly into the camera so that it can be edited into the interview. It is a standard process, and the repeat questions are called 'cutaways'. It is essential to have cutaways if a film is to be edited without unpleasant jump-cuts of the face of the person being interviewed.

It may look odd, after the interview proper is over, to see the reporter firing questions into thin air and looking very serious at the same time. What *you* should be doing is standing close to the reporter to **make sure that the questions are the same as the ones put in the actual interview.** Sometimes it's a question of reporters forgetting the precise wording of the interview questions; but very occasionally unscrupulous reporters will alter their questions during cutaways, in order to harden them up or significantly change their emphasis. This can be unfair if it alters the way your answer comes over. If you have given your answer in response to a question A in the interview, but on screen the reporter asks a question B, then clearly your answer may not fit:

Question A: 'What are the next steps you plan?'
Answer: 'It's difficult to say. We shall have to look at the situation when the committee meets tomorrow and decide where to go from here.'
Question B: 'Wouldn't it be true to say that you haven't the faintest idea what to do next?'

When the cutaway question B is edited into the film, it subtly distorts the meaning and effect of the answer.

To be fair, some reporters simply change a question in a cutaway to make it shorter and more to the point. In that case, your answer will have precisely the same impact as if it were still replying to the original question. Listen to the cutaways being done. **If you do hear what strikes you as an unfair question, say so loudly.** Do it while the cutaways are being done and tell the reporter that he/she is inventing a question that he/she did not ask you. If you stand close enough to the microphone you can go on spoiling the cutaways for ever until the reporter does ask the same questions as those put in the interview.

Studio interviews

■ **Sit comfortably.** Sitting in a studio needs care. You should be relaxed but upright in your seat. Do not slump. Be alert. Leave your hands casually in your lap, and don't wave them about during the interview (quite natural use of the hands and arms to emphasise a point in normal conversation can, on television, make you look like a naval cadet practising semaphore). Don't swivel in the chair but use your head and shoulders to make a point. Remember the need to use the whole face and eyes to project yourself.

■ **Do not take notes into the studio.** You should have the facts and arguments on the tip of your tongue. You can take in a specific document or object in order to hold it up to prove a point. But do not read from anything unless it is an extremely dramatic and significant sentence of thirty words or less. Instead, you can say, 'What this document/letter/newspaper cutting shows quite conclusively is . . .', and then say it in your own words.

■ **Don't smoke** – having you lighting up a cigarette or pipe is horribly distracting for the viewer.

■ **Keep an eye on the clock.** Try to have an idea of how the time is going. Always find out beforehand how long the interview or discussion is going to last. It is worth keeping your watch cupped in your hand so that, when you are not speaking (this applies only in discussions, not one-to-one interviews), you can glance at the time. The point is to ensure that you finish off with a bang (or, where there are two or more people in a discussion, that you are the last speaker), and that the interviewer does not have to interrupt you in the middle of a sentence because time has run out.

Watch out for the studio manager's time signals to the interviewer. The studio manager will guide you to your seat and stand just to the side of one of the cameras, in direct eye-line with the interviewer during the interview or discussion. It is by watching the studio manager that the interviewer knows how much time he has left. When there is one minute to go, the studio manager will hold up one finger; with 30 seconds to go, he or she will hold up his/her arms in the shape of a St Andrews

Cross. The sign that it is time to wrap up is the forearm, or just the wrist and hand, going round in circles; and the sign that the interview or discussion must be terminated, no matter who is speaking, is known as 'the cut-throat' – the side of the hand being moved backwards and forwards across the studio manager's throat. The signs to look for are the one-minute or 30-seconds sign, and the circular motion meaning time to draw to a close. That is when you should be ready to seize control of the interview or discussion and get in a punchy final point. If you steam into a final point *after* the wrap-up sign, make it a very short one indeed. If you start talking at length, the interviewer will get the cut-throat sign and will be forced to interrupt you and finish the interview.

One of television's better performers, Tony Benn, was once asked to be the other guest in a two-headed discussion on a current-affairs programme in the regions. When he arrived, he asked the producer how long the interview would be. The producer said, 'About three or four minutes, we'll see how it goes.' Benn insisted that he wanted to know the exact length, since he understood that all programmes – above all, the regional 6.00 p.m. programmes, which have to knit together their film pieces, studio interviews and news clips particularly carefully – have a tight schedule in which the allotted time for a discussion is very precise. The producer told him that the planned time was in fact 3 minutes 45 seconds.

Benn went into the studio with his watch in the palm of his hand. He took a full part in the discussion. Then, with only 25 seconds to go, he intervened directly into what the other person was saying, with 'Look, what we're all forgetting is . . .' He spoke until exactly 3 minutes 41 seconds were up, leaving the interviewer with time only to bring the interview to an immediate end.

Remote studio interviews

Sometimes you will be asked to do a television interview 'down the line' – when you have to go and sit in a studio, listen to the questions through an earphone and deliver your answers into a camera. Perhaps the most common programme to use this method is *Nationwide*, which regularly has the London presenter interviewing people sitting in the Leeds or Glasgow studio. To the viewer at home it looks as if everyone is face-to-face.

The usual rules for interviews apply here too:

■ treat the camera you are looking at as if it were a human being

■ react *with your face* to the interviewer's questions

■ when answering, imagine you are next to him or her in person.

If you are taking part in a discussion from a remote studio, do not be put off by your physical isolation from the other participants. Use exactly the same techniques as you would in an ordinary studio interview – cut in, talk directly to other participants. In doing so, you will ensure they do not forget you just because you are not present in person.

Getting cash from television

Television news and current affairs coverage is costly. The early 1979 budget for *TV Eye* was £17,000 for each half-hour programme – and that doesn't include the salaries of the staff who work to produce it.

Television researchers, reporters and producers are used to paying out sums of cash to help smooth their work and to persuade people to provide the required information or be interviewed.

Whenever a television producer phones up Enoch Powell, for example, one of the first questions Powell asks is: 'What will the fee be?' And he may not appear if the fee is too low.

Football personalities also play this game effectively. When Tommy Docherty was sacked by Aston Villa in 1969, a BBC regional-television producer in Birmingham wanted him to come in that very night and be interviewed in a special half-hour programme. Docherty demanded £200 in cash before he agreed. He got it.

In fact, most of the politicians and trade-union leaders you see in the studios are earning cash from the BBC or ITV for their appearances. Some, who are thought to be 'good value' by television producers, can set their own fees.

■ **Studio interviews.** The rule is that, if you go into a studio to be interviewed, the television company will pay you a fee plus expenses. It is worth asking about this beforehand – reminding the company, if necessary, of the money you will lose giving up work for half a day or even a couple of hours, and the inconvenience involved. However, **you do not get** – and it is pointless asking for them – **fees for short news interviews,** even on the national television news programmes.

Minimum fees

6.00 p.m. regional programme	£10
Nationwide	£25
Weekend World	£40

If you don't ask for your fee in advance, you may get less than you should. Don't be shy. Everyone in television is used to politicians asking about their fees; the sums involved are tiny compared with the money spent daily on taxis by a busy television office; and few television journalists, at any level, have qualms about spending their bosses' money. The money can be a useful contribution to a dispute fund.

■ **Documentaries.** Appearing in a documentary is different. If a producer wants to come and film you or interview you, it is important to get the terms right first. If the producer or researcher has approached you, rather than the other way round, it means that they badly need you for the programme. You should **ask for a contract in advance,** and make sure you negotiate fees and expenses you are happy with.

A contract sounds a bit like big business, but all television programmes using non-staff people – actors, musicians, celebrities, politicians, *you* – pay them by way of a contract. Even if you get only £10 for appearing on a 6.00 p.m. regional news programme, it will be accompanied by a retrospective contract.

A mean-minded producer may try and fob you off by saying that he doesn't deal with money, and tell you to contact the Contracts Department. Don't be put off. Get him to put in writing what the fee and expenses will be.

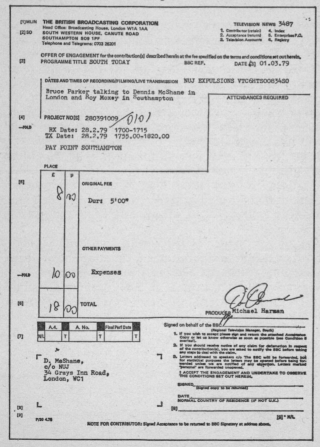

A regional television interview contract

■ **Research fees.** As well as fees for appearing on television, you can charge fees for research – and you should so charge for any special information that a producer or researcher asks you for. Inside information on a strike, background to a dispute, finding people to appear in a film – all these count as research.

You have to judge when to ask for a research fee. If you are trying to build a relationship with the regional newsrooms it will not be helped if you gain a name as someone who always demands cash before passing over information. But if a London-based producer or researcher whom you will never see again comes along asking for help, then you should ask for something in return.

■ **Facility fees.** You can make a charge if a television news crew uses your office, workplace or home for the purposes of filming. It's a kind of hire charge and also covers the use of electricity, the cups of tea you make for the crew, the mess they leave behind and the slight damage caused by humping a lot of electrical equipment through a room.

During lengthy news events like the Grunwick dispute, television news crews take over rooms at good vantage-spots and pay up to £50 a day to the owners of well-placed houses.

Facility fees are not a con. A documentary film crew can completely disrupt the ground floor of a house, take up considerable time and leave a lot of mess behind. You deserve the facility fee. Institutions that are used to film crews – churches, Pall Mall clubs, Oxbridge colleges – have always asked for, and got, big facility fees.

Again, it is a matter of judgement. You can't expect a one-man regional freelance cameraman, shooting a silent news film of a meeting, to pay a facility fee; but, if a producer from *World In Action* asks to film a trades council executive committee meeting for a general programme, then demand a facility fee. It will be paid.

At the time of fourteen-year-old Timothy Davey's arrest and trial in Turkey on drugs charges, he was interviewed for 30 minutes by Thames TV. The company contributed £1,000 to his defence fund.

10.

Dealing with radio

Radio journalists / handling interviews /
being a phone-in guest

Radio journalists

Like television and press newsrooms, radio newsrooms
have **reporters** working to a **news editor** who selects the stories.
The current-affairs programmes are run by **producers** who decide
upon and set up interviews. Some programmes, such as Radio 4's
Today or LBC's *A.M.*, have regular **presenters** who link together
the different items and do some interviews themselves.

Radio news coverage and programme interviews have to be
planned well in advance just like other news output in newspapers and television.

Handling interviews

The discipline of a radio interview is similar to that of a
television interview (see pages 135ff.). The same techniques apply.
You have to work out in advance what you want to say, choose
two or three main points, use vivid language and, above all,
project yourself.

There are two advantages in radio:

■ you can hold a note in your hand to remind yourself of
the main points you wish to cover (but **don't read from a piece of
paper,** because that comes over as sounding wooden)

■ radio is far more flexible: **if you are doing a recorded
interview** – at the studio, into a tape-recorder or over the phone –
never, never, be shy of asking to do it again.

The following checkpoints assume that yours *will* be a
recorded interview. In most cases, the practical advice (about
being courteous to the interviewer, thinking carefully about
what you're going to say, not making unnecessary noise that will

be picked up by the microphone, etc.) applies to all interviews, live or recorded. However, **in live interviews there isn't the chance to go back and begin again** – so be doubly careful. (See page 162 following for special tips on **telephone interviews, studio interviews, remote studios** and **being a phone-in guest.**)

Decide what you want to say. In radio, rather more than in television, the person being interviewed is expected to explain the story. A common introduction on a local-radio news bulletin will be:

> 'Hospital workers and nurses at Perth General Hospital have staged a lightning walk-out in protest at the dismissal of their branch chairman. The union involved is COHSE, the Confederation of Health Service Employees. Jack Smith asked their regional secretary about the reasons for the strike.'

In cases like this, you will have to be able to boil down the history of a dispute and the reasons for whatever has happened into a couple of sentences.

You can always try to protect yourself by saying:

> This is a complex situation which can't be explained in a couple of sentences, but if there is basically one reason it is because . . .'

But, when it comes to editing the tape, most reporters and producers won't be at all keen to start the interview in this vein. For one thing, they think listeners get bored if people start talking about 'complex situations'. And in any case, journalists (especially those in radio) pride themselves precisely on being able to explain *anything* in a couple of sentences. **So the razor blade and editing block will come out and, in answer to the question implied by the introduction ('the reasons for the strike'), you will appear to begin by saying 'Because . . .' – and your qualifying first phrase about complexity is lost.**

It is better to start off sharply, with a single 'wrap-up' sentence:

> 'This strike is about blind bureaucracy gone mad. One of the nurses – our branch secretary – refused to obey a bureaucrat's order to close up a ward and was dismissed because she prefers patients to the petty tyrants in hospital

administration. But really, this is just the culmination of two years' refusal by the administrators to have proper discussion with the nurses and other staff about how best to look after the patients.'

This way you get the background in, but as a support for a sharp opening; and the razor-happy producer is unlikely to cut either point.

■ Keep your answers short. In the first place, this makes unfriendly editing more difficult. It also allows the momentum of an interview to gather pace. This gives the interview and what you say in it more impact.

■ Identify your purpose and your audience. This is not as obvious as it seems. Depending on your judgement of other media coverage, and of the current situation, your purpose in a radio interview can vary considerably. For example:

■ you may want to get your side of the story across in the face of slanted press coverage – (a)

■ you may want to inspire sympathetic action from members elsewhere – (b)

■ you may want to enhance the image of your union – (c).

So, go back to our imaginary hospital strike. If you decide that the main purpose is (a), you might emphasise during the interview that the full facts are not available, that your members have been harassed by the local press and that, with their highly paid PROs, the health authority always get their side of the story over. If (b), you can say you are contacting trades-council leaders, or local T&GWU officials to stop deliveries, and that the strike could spread to other hospitals. If (c), point out how reluctant your members were to strike, emphasise that the union is fighting for the patients and make clear that patients will not suffer.

You must also decide what audience you are chiefly aiming at. Are you:

■ speaking to members of your union not involved in the issue?

■ speaking to 'trade unionists' and active supporters?

■ speaking to the public at large?

■ warning other employers or isolating the employer concerned?

■ speaking to the management with whom you are in dispute?

Again, you tailor your replies to the audience. All sorts of phrases can be used to bring in points aimed at specific audiences:

■ 'This issue is much wider than this factory. It concerns every trade unionist in the area.'

■ 'I think electricians, members of the EETPU, everywhere in the city will be very angry when they hear what's happened.'

■ 'I'm not sure the public realise what's going on here. If the general public knew the full facts we'd have their total sympathy.'

■ 'Look – this management seem to want another Grunwick. The kind of industrial action they are provoking will lead to a very bitter dispute that could spread out well beyond the firm.'

■ 'The men and women are very angry and determined. They'll stay out for as long as is necessary. We've contacted most of the other unions in town and this place won't be able to operate before long.'

But never, never, never make any threat in a radio interview that you cannot deliver.

■ **Try to understand the news editor's or producer's problems.** If a big story breaks, radio can get on to it faster than any other medium – but the news editor cannot assume that big stories will break at convenient times. Every morning he/she has to sit down, sift the diary, look at the press releases, see what is in the local press or what local stories are in the national press, make sure his or her reporters have done calls to the police, firestations and other regular contacts – and then construct the main news bulletins for lunch- and tea-time. The reporters have to be sent out/told what stories to start getting telephone interviews on/told which people to get into the studio for an interview.

As with all the other media, therefore, the more advance notice you give the better. Be alive to the problems of radio deadlines. It is no use if asked for an interview at 2.00 p.m. to offer 5.00 p.m. instead, because by 5.00 p.m. the main tea-time news programme will almost certainly have been structured, with interviews already slotted in.

■ **For local radio, keep it local and immediate.** Radio Leeds, for example, is unlikely to be interested in a national NUBE story unless local banks are directly affected. A test of immediacy is to see whether or not you can work the word 'today' into it: not 'teachers in Kent's primary schools are angry over delays in cutting down class sizes', but 'teachers in Kent have today sent a

message of protest to local education chiefs because of delays . . .'
In fact, that is one of the simplest ways of making news immediate: send a letter (to anyone – Prime Minister, General Secretary, Council leader, managing director) about the issue you
want publicity for and then tell the radio station and the other
media about it. Better still, send them a copy of the letter with an
embargo on it saying, 'not for use until 10.00 a.m. Monday' – the
time when the letter is expected to arrive. (If you do this, **always
make it clear in the letter that you are releasing it.** A common
sentence is: 'Because of the great concern about this issue I am
making this letter available to my members and the public.')
Remember, 'immediacy' can stretch only to yesterday, or what
will happen tomorrow – beyond that, we are in the realms of
ancient history or the uncharted future.

If you are talking about a national action, always talk in
terms of its effect on local factories or institutions. Throw in the
names of local factories, localities and companies.

■ **Be friendly, and as helpful as possible.** Don't begin by
being hostile to the interviewer before the recording starts.
Ninety-nine out of a 100 radio reporters are not interested in
doing you down. Their interest is in making the most of the
story, in bringing back 'good radio' with plenty of impact.

Take time to explain the background. A lot of radio reporting is the straight voice-piece, or a report with odd bits of
interview cut into it. If you have any written material you are
providing for newspaper reporters, or leaflets for members, send
them to the radio reporter. **Never assume that the reporter knows
enough about an issue.**

However complicated the story is, the reporter in nearly all
cases has got to do the interview with you in a maximum of three
and a half minutes; and he or she will be lucky to get all of that
on air. Don't blame the reporter for the lack of time: accept it,
and structure your replies accordingly.

Try and be positive. Don't say, 'I don't know.' Say, 'We
haven't considered that yet' or, 'It's a very difficult situation and
any comment I might make on that will only make it far worse.'
But be ready to speculate: 'The men are very angry and there is
very strong pressure for a strike' or, 'It will be for the district
committee to decide, but there's a fair chance they will order
some kind of action.'

Local radio often comes back for more. If you do an effective interview and if you get on with the reporter, you will be
remembered as someone to come back to if the dispute or issue

continues or develops. Someone who gives a good interview will even be remembered beyond the immediate issue.

It is not simply a question of providing good answers. It is more to do with enthusiasm, with being prepared to be interviewed at any time and to shape the length of answers to what is needed, and with taking a friendly approach to the radio journalist who makes the contact.

> Listeners to Radio Birmingham often used to hear reporters interviewing a particular Tory councillor. In or out of office, he was always ready to be interviewed and provided good solid Conservative opinions on any council subject. He was used a lot, and the no-nonsense image he projected helped him become a Tory parliamentary candidate in the city and, eventually, an MP.
>
> The opposite was often the case with Labour representatives. Even reporters personally sympathetic to Labour found it difficult to persuade their comrades to be interviewed and to explain the stories in which they were involved. Their suspicion may be understandable. But their attitude only meant that their case went by default.

■ **Be careful with figures.** Never be tempted to fudge the exact amounts involved in a money dispute. If cash is at issue – whether it is the weekly wage, the hourly rate, a bonus rate, take-home pay, a percentage increase claimed or offered – **always give the exact amount.** Any rounding up or down and the management (and possibly your own colleagues) can accurately denounce you for putting out inaccurate information. Even if the inaccuracy is in the interests of comprehension (e.g., 'around £3 a day', instead of '£3.13p') those opposed to you can accuse you of being misleading.

The same is true of numbers generally. It is safer to say, 'All 483 women will be involved', rather than 'About 500 women will be involved'. It is quite likely that, if the radio journalist is writing a news item or an introduction, *he or she* will say 'About 500 women . . .'; but *you* should try to get the *precise* number in, at the beginning, even if you use the generalisation 'about 500' later on in the interview. This is vital in disputes to do with recognition or organisation, when you and the employer will be playing the numbers game. Any inaccuracy will only help the employer.

When other people are indirectly involved, outside your direct area of control and concern, then obviously you cannot be expected to be exact with the numbers involved. It is perfectly reasonable for you to say, 'More than 1,000 people will be affected in the factory if the maintenance men walk out' or, 'There are about 400 patients in the hospital who could be affected because of the bureaucrats' refusal to talk to us' or, 'About 3,000 school children may have to be sent home if teachers go ahead with their protest action.'

■ **Don't be rude.** It never pays to be rude and argumentative. Most listeners will side with the person who is attacked, not with the aggressor. If an interviewer is being unfair to you, the listener's sympathy will be with you; but, if you go rudely on the offensive, his sympathy will switch.

> In a studio confrontation on LBC between the National Front's Martin Webster and Dr Mervyn Stockwood, Bishop of Woolwich, Dr Stockwood lost his temper and was rude to Webster. Several days later, when talking to an LBC journalist, Webster said he had received an enormously sympathetic postbag – not because of his views, but because of the offensive way he had been treated by the Bishop!

You can't win if you are argumentative in a recorded interview. If you *lose* the point, the interviewer will leave it in – because anger makes good radio and your losing the point makes the interviewer look good. If you *win* the argument, the interviewer will cut it out – because, although it still makes for good radio, it also makes him look foolish.

By all means be rude about the employer, the government, your own union, the local newspaper and anything else you like. Use colourful language too – but remember that the strongest swear-word likely to be broadcast is 'bloody', and even that as little as possible! In any case, once in an interview will do. Too common a use of an expletive lessens its dramatic impact.

Within these limits, an expletive can usefully convey the anger contained in a situation:

Question: What is your reaction to the management decision?
Answer: It's bloody disgraceful.

This can make a good start to an interview if the situation demands a strong public reaction from the union.

■ **Avoid jargon.** One trade union's or industry's jargon can be meaningless to trade unionists in another union or industry. More to the point, much trade-union jargon – and some of the language of politics generally – means very little to people whose lives are not centred around these activities. Most people know what TUC stands for (or, at least, what it represents) – but can everyone translate NEC, JNC, NJNC, Confed, etc.?

It is often better to say, for example, 'We shall have to negotiate this nationally now', rather than 'The matter will be referred to the Joint National Council'.

■ **Don't be embarrassed by your mistakes.** Even with lots of preparation and, with luck, a good amount of experience, you will still make mistakes. Sometimes words will come out jumbled up. Perhaps you will get a figure wrong. Quite often it is the common phenomenon of the tongue being slightly in advance of the brain – you don't say the words you intended to say. If anything like this happens, don't worry – unless you are being interviewed live. **Go back to where you started and begin all over again.**

If what you *mean* to say is, 'This dispute could go on for months, but that isn't likely because of the effects our action is having in the Coventry factory . . .', but what you *actually* say is, 'This dispute could go on for months but that is likely because of the effect . . .' – then **stop,** say to the interviewer, 'Sorry, I've got that wrong' and go straight on to say the sentence you meant to say, without pause. The reporter's razor blade will cut out your fluff and apology when he gets back to the studio.

Drying up is also quite common. You'd be surprised at the famous broadcasters who do it. If your mind goes blank, just let the tape run on while you wait to get going again. If you want to stop altogether and have a moment to think and get yourself into gear again, then say, 'Hang on a second, can we do that bit again.'

■ **Go somewhere quiet.** It is always better to do a radio interview in the quietest place possible. Extraneous sounds on tape will only spoil the impact of what you're saying. The interviewer him/herself will probably mention the need to have silence during a recording, but it's just as well if you already take that for granted. At a news conference, for example, it is wise to have a side room ready for radio interviews. In a trade-union office, you may have to ask secretaries to stop typing in the next office because their noise will drown the interview. Out of doors, it may be necessary to go and sit in a car.

Telephone interviews

All radio newsrooms now make extensive use of interviews done over the telephone. Quite often the request to do a telephone interview will be made early in the morning or late in the evening, when you are at home. You may not be as fully prepared as if the reporter had given you advance warning, so remember – **you can always ask the journalist to phone back** in a few minutes, so that you can prepare yourself for the interview, jot down the main points and gear yourself up to put them over effectively.

Studio interviews

Virtually the same rules apply as for television interviews (see pages 149ff.), except that you won't be asked to make up and the last time a colleague of mine was interviewed on BBC Radio London he was asked to pay for his cup of coffee! (There is next to no money in BBC local radio and you will rarely get a drink, let alone a fee when you go to the studio for an interview. However, local radio will pay for transport – a taxi to and from the studio, for example – and, with its increasing profitability, commercial radio is now in a position to pay fees for substantial studio contributions – for example, if you are a guest on a **phone-in** programme.)

Radio studios aren't as outlandish as television ones. Most interviews are done around a plain table, with a microphone either suspended from the ceiling or sticking through a hole in the middle of the table. (You might find yourself being interviewed in front of an alarming control console: just concentrate on talking to the interviewer.) **Don't turn away from the microphone when you're speaking,** because then your voice won't carry.

Stay still, **don't** rustle papers, **don't** let your knees knock or rub the surface of the table, **don't** hit it to emphasise a point, **don't** light a match or blow your nose or click a ball-point pen. **All these sounds, which we're used to ignoring in normal conversation, will be picked up by the microphone as quite dreadful thumps and clicks** – rustling paper, particularly, can sound like a waterfall! If you must blow your nose, or cough, or light a match, wait for a suitable moment and then turn away from the microphone (taking care not to kick the table, as it will come over as a terrible clump).

In all broadcast discussions, radio or television, you have to be ready to talk directly to other participants – if necessary, across the presenter. **In a radio discussion, if you do want to cut into someone else's chatter, do so decisively and seize control of the discussion.** Two people talking across each other sounds completely unintelligible on the radio. On television the audience can see people's faces and tell where the different voices are coming from; radio forces the listener to rely solely on the evidence of his or her ears, which is much more difficult. If you do intervene, do so with a very strong point which forces the others to give way.

Conversely, if you are in a spoiling mood, you can refuse to be put down or interrupted yourself by carrying on speaking in a determined manner. The professional interviewer or presenter will realise that it sounds like garbled nonsense on air, and so will give way to you and allow you to finish your point!

Remote studios

If a national BBC Radio programme wants to use you, it is quite likely that you will have to go to a local radio station or to a regional-radio centre and be interviewed 'down the line'. The BBC also has remotely controlled studios, which have to be operated by the person being interviewed. These can be in bizarre places – underneath a football stand or, in Coventry, in the Cathedral crypt.

If you have to go to a remote studio, you will be given precise instructions on how to get there and what to do when you arrive. Give yourself a little extra time as it may take a few moments to read all the printed instructions on the door or table which tell you how to work the equipment. Don't worry if you get mixed up. There is always a telephone which connects directly to the control room in London and, if you have not made contact after the allotted time, the producer or engineer will come through on the phone and explain what to do.

The technique is similar to remote television interviews. In a discussion with others, **be ready to come in with your point without waiting to be asked. The chairman cannot see you** and, once the first question and answer (which acts as a voice introduction for the participants) is over, **it is very much up to you to intervene as you think best.**

Being a phone-in guest

More and more trade-union representatives are being asked in as guests for phone-in programmes, and it is as well to bring the idea up with a phone-in producer if your own union is in the news.

The technique is a little different from participating in other radio interviews or discussions:

■ You will be given a pair of earphones, through which you hear the questions. Ask for a pad of paper and take brief notes while the questioner is speaking.

■ Even if the question annoys you, try to be conciliatory. Remember that, although thousands of people are listening, most of them are doing so in the privacy of their homes or cars and probably on their own. A loud or over-authoritative guest makes a poor impression.

■ Don't worry too much about producing short, snappy answers – treat the business as a gentle conversation. A phone-in programme is the one occasion when the general broadcasting rule about projecting yourself is not essential (although, of course, you should keep alert).

■ If you are invited to be a phone-in guest, you can ask colleagues to listen in and phone up with a friendly question. It does not have to be pro-union. It can be about a firm's profits, about government policy, about a piece of news that will provide a peg to make a good point.

■ Flatter your questioners. Start off by saying 'That's a very good question' or, 'That's an interesting point' – but then go on gently to rebut any hostile arguments and make your own point.

11.

Putting your point of view directly

Letters to the editor / phone-ins / access
programmes and columns

Letters to the editor

All newspapers and magazines carry a letters column, and
letters columns are widely read. Yet people organising a campaign or running a dispute often forget about them when planning media coverage.

A good letter can be a spur to a news editor to initiate news
coverage of the points mentioned.

The letters column should also be used to put over general
political points. Here is an excellent letter that appeared in the
Observer in the week following publication of a long article by a
retired general predicting a Third World War for 1985. The
article was a crude propaganda job for increased military spending, but the message was effectively destroyed in the letter:

> Dear Sir,
> My newsagent delivered me a 25-year-old copy of the
> *Observer* last Sunday. Admittedly the dateline was correct,
> but internal evidence demonstrates that General Sir John
> Hackett's extract from the *Third World War* – Britain's
> Hiroshima 1985 – was in fact written at the height of the
> Cold War.
>
> It is a great pity that the *Observer*, which in recent years
> has rejected the role of mouthpiece for Foreign Office and
> Army hardliners, should have suffered this time-warp.
> General Hackett, who obviously enjoys military things,
> should confine his retirement to drilling private armies on
> Surbiton golf course.
>
> Yours,
> Roderick Clyne

■ You do not need the apocalyptic prophecies of a retired general to spur you into writing a letter. In particular, when there is an important newsworthy strike in which the trade unionists involved are being hammered by the media, others workers not directly involved should **write letters of support** to the local press.

■ Officials or branch secretaries can write draft letters for other members to sign. There is nothing unethical in this. In many cases, a letter appearing in *The Times* over the signature of a trade-union general secretary will have been written by some head-office official. If you write to a government minister, you may receive a signed personal reply – but you can bet that the letter was written by a civil servant. It is, therefore, quite proper to produce a draft for someone else to sign. Of course, the person doing the signing must agree first, and he or she must be free to amend the draft in any way.

■ If possible, **type the letter,** or write it out in block capitals. **Use one side of the paper only. Be conscious of deadlines** (letters columns tend to get sub-edited and set in type fairly early in the production process). For a weekly paper, it is wisest to get the letter to the office on the Monday of the week the paper appears. For an evening paper, the morning of the day before is a safe deadline.

■ Letters can be very short. Here is one from a miner's wife in Wales, written to the *Sunday Mirror*:

> If miners work less overtime, as one reader suggests, how will it help those on the dole?
>
> Anyway, I would like to meet the miner who is taking home £100 a week.
>
> My husband doesn't after six days down the pit.'

That is a perfect form for a letter denying a newspaper report of high wages. **False claims that workers are earning high wages can and should always be denied,** and the best denial comes from the worker's partner who is more likely than anyone else to know how much hard cash is coming into the household.

■ Letters to the editor are a useful way of keeping an issue in the public eye.

The Lucas Aerospace Combine Shop Stewards' Committee produced a detailed, well-researched plan to show how they could gradually become less dependent on defence-industry work and start making socially useful (and still profitable) products. The committee needed publicity for the plan, and in different ways got it. Many of the people who supported the plan took advantage of stories about it to write follow-up letters. Here is a letter which appeared in *Labour Weekly*:

> I wish to put the story in *Labour Weekly* about government intervention at Lucas Aerospace in perspective.
>
> On 16 March this year (1978), the company announced that it would be making 2,000 people redundant over the next two years, 1,500 of them at Victor Works, Liverpool. The new factory at Huyton will employ only 500 people, less than a third of those made redundant at Liverpool. And there is a very great fear that the jobs at Huyton will not go to those made redundant at Victor Works, who have very different skills, but will go to other employees in the company, and that there is no guarantee that the company will stay at Huyton beyond the end of the rent-free period of five years.
>
> The Government's speed in providing aid of £8 million to Lucas Aerospace with very few strings attached contrasts markedly with their refusal to assist the Lucas Aerospace Combine Shop Stewards' Committee, who warned over two years ago that the company was planning heavy redundancies and who drew up a plan for 150 socially useful products which could be made by the company.
>
> This plan would save many more jobs and ensure that the country got a range of worthwhile products in exchange for its investment in Lucas Aerospace.

This letter makes its points well and keeps up the pressure on the Labour government to take up seriously the proposals from the Combine Committee.

Quality papers like *The Times* like printing letters from shop stewards, especially if they make their position clear in the text of the letter ('Writing as a shop steward for the past five years . . .' or, 'As someone who has worked in a factory all my life, can I say . . .') – because the editors think that it shows how broadly based the readership is and that it makes a change from the usual middle-class, professional and establishment letters that they receive and publish. *The Times* letters column is a very important platform. It is read by many of the people who wield real power in the country. It is taken very seriously by the paper and will often print letters arguing the labour and trade-union movement point of view.

■ Another way to increase the impact of a letter and give it more chance of being published is to get lots of signatures to it. Any letters-column editor will be impressed if a letter has several signatures – if nothing else, he knows all *those* people will buy the paper to see if their letter is published! You can type your letter (or write it out in block capitals) and then get your mates at work or at a branch meeting to sign it. Make sure they *print* their names as well as writing their signatures, so that the sub-editor has no problem deciphering the scrawl.

Phone-ins

It ought to be the easiest thing in the world to take part in a phone-in. You simply dial the number given, wait your turn and then ask your question or make your point. Why then are phone-ins sometimes so embarrassing to listen to? People stumble and are hesitant, get rudely put down by the presenter and, in general terms, the views you hear seem to be anchored firmly right of centre.

It is true that workers do not have such easy access to a telephone as middle-class people have, and they are likely to be at work anyway when most phone-ins are broadcast. None the less, the trade-union argument should not go by default.

If your union is in the news, you should encourage colleagues who will be at home (or perhaps their husbands or wives, or other members of the family) to listen to the phone-in and join in.

A radio set should be a mandatory piece of equipment in union offices so that officers can listen to local news reports to see how their case is being presented and join in phone-ins to put over the trade-union point of view. It need not be the regional secretary or local convenor. The office secretary or clerk can take part, or perhaps a visiting member.

You can – and, at times, should – **organise a phone-in campaign.** Ask half-a-dozen members to try to participate in a particular day's phone-in and argue the same case in their different ways. If a known enemy of the Labour movement is the phone-in guest – a right-wing Tory or the local CBI representative – make sure members are told to ring in with hard questions. This may seem like unfair manipulation, but at election times all the main parties tell their organisers to arrange for articulate party members to phone in with penetrating questions for phone-in guest politicians. Similarly, the National Front organises its members to try and hog certain phone-ins at certain times.

Never try and read out a question or general contribution into the telephone: it will always sound stilted. Keep the question short. Don't cram more than one or two points into each contribution. Be aggressive or courteous, depending on how you want to put over your point. Don't be frightened to say that something is untrue or rubbish, if that is the case.

Often you may have to wait a while until the special phone-in number is answered. Keep hanging on: the calls get answered in strict first-come-first-served rotation. Once the studio producer has answered, you may find him or her asking you about the question or point you want to put. **Be careful not to tell them if you are going to put an identical question or point of view to one that has already been broadcast.**

Make sure the radio is turned down when you are due to go on air. If you try to listen to yourself on the radio at the same time as you are speaking down the telephone, the little microphone in the telephone handset will pick up the radio sound and a terrible noise called 'howlround' will then get broadcast.

Commercial local radio stations have a seven-second tape-delay system, in order to bleep out any profanity or stop someone saying something libellous (see page 176). The BBC does not operate a tape-delay system, which means you can say what you like. However, there is not much point in swearing and, if you say something libellous and someone knows who you are, then you can be sued just as if you wrote the libel in a newspaper.

Access programmes and columns

A significant development in the media in the 1970s has been the opening of airwaves and newspaper columns to people wanting to put their point of view directly without being filtered through a journalist's typewriter.

Television

The BBC TV series called *Open Door* was followed up by several ITV companies, notably LWT and Granada, who began similar programmes. At the same time, *The Sunday Times* launched its 'Opinion' page (or rather, half page!), which has three pieces from non-journalists published each week.

Cynics have dismissed these access spots as mere public relations on the part of the media, designed to give an impression of greater public participation and to head off criticisms that the public had been denied access, especially in the monopoly area of television. There may be some truth in this – certainly, these access programmes are broadcast at times when the audience is very low. The fact remains that they are there and trade-union members and other groups which do not have automatic media access could use them to get over their message.

The access programmes vary enormously. Some place a film crew at the disposal of the outside group. Others have participants come in and read a two- or three-minute piece straight to camera. To make a longer programme, it is necessary to set about it professionally.

The first thing that the access producers look for in a group pressing for space or time is that it should be representative and have something to say. A single shop steward is unlikely to be given 30 minutes to him/herself, but a joint unions' committee might convince the producers that they do represent a broad base of opinion.

It will be necessary to show how the programme will be put together, what facts or ideas will be spelled out, who will be speaking and what graphs, maps or visual aids will be used. All the research and documentation compiled should be sent in with the application. If you have made contact with a producer or researcher in television, ask him or her to help in formulating the application.

The press

In newspapers or magazines, it is just a question of writing the article to the length specified. However, writing anything takes time and care. Don't put off getting down to the physical act of writing – once you've begun it is easier to keep going. The first two sentences are always the killers; after that the problem is often to keep it down to the number of words allowed.

When you get stuck – and everyone, even the professional writer, has moments, before or during the writing of a piece, when nothing seems to be in the mind and available for transfer to the page – look at a story or feature in one of the day's newspapers and try constructing a sentence, or paragraph or whole piece along the lines of what you've read. Obviously, the facts and opinions are yours; but the *structure* can be borrowed. Anyway, if you pick an approach from another article and it unlocks the block in your mind, you will probably find that you can get going again and that your piece will develop in your own original style.

Radio

■ **In local radio,** apart from phone-ins, there is another type of access: when the radio station gives a regular programme over to an outside group, who then make it themselves. A common example in BBC local radio is church programmes produced by local councils of churches.

Some stations have given monthly half-hour programmes to local trades councils to use as they wish:

> BBC Radio Nottingham had one such programme, run by a couple of interested full-time officials These officials had interviews on tape with local trade unionists in the news and with visiting trade-union leaders, live studio discussions about local and national trade-union issues, reports on trades-council meetings, discussions about new legislation that affected trade unions – in short, this was a chatty, lively magazine-format programme, under the exclusive control of the trades council. Radio Nottingham's contribution was to provide the loan of a tape recorder for outside recordings, technical studio assistance and, most important of all, half an hour of broadcasting time.

■ **Commercial radio stations** are less likely to prove co-operative – firstly, because they would have problems in fitting in advertisements and, secondly, because the Independent Broadcasting Authority would be very uneasy about surrendering editorial control to an outside body. Still, there are ways round both problems and it would be worth suggesting such programmes as an idea to the local-station management.

Producing a radio programme takes time. A 15-minute magazine containing two or three taped interviews, a discussion and a report of the last trades-council meeting can take up two evenings (for recording the interviews), a couple of hours on the phone (for fixing up the studio discussion), half an hour doing the trades-council report, and three or four hours at the studio for editing the tape and recording the programme. The station will show outsiders how to use the tape recorder and how to edit (both of which are easy with a little practice), but the ideas, energy and commitment will have to come from the individuals who want to make the programme.

12.

Complaints

Importance of complaints / libel / the Press
Council / complaints about broadcasting /
other methods of complaint

Importance of complaints

Complaining about *bad* media coverage is a vital part of
the process of getting *good* media coverage. The reason is simple.
Journalists live in a news vacuum, in which they have little contact with the people who are the objects of their coverage. Journalists criticise each other – and when the criticism comes down the
newsroom hierarchy it can be fiercely vicious – but they do so
using journalistic criteria that do not have a direct relation to the
situation portrayed in the story. For example, a news editor will
tongue-lash a reporter for not writing as the intro to the story
the fact that six people were arrested at a mass picket – when, in
fact, the most important aspect of the event was the massive
turn-out and the closure of the factory. The other side of this is
that journalists in a newsroom concerned with manufacturing a
newspaper or programme have no way of checking whether or
not the report that is brought back is a full, accurate and balanced
account of the event. Almost by definition, if a single reporter
produces a story then no other journalist is in a position to judge
its accuracy and fairness.

That is why it is so important, if a story is wrong – whether
through inaccuracy, distortion or unfairness – that the journalists
be told so. If they are not told, they will believe they got it right;
the individual journalist as well as his colleagues will consider
that she/he has told the truth and will base future stories on the
assumption that the account is accurate.

A letter of factual correction, or one pointing out unfairness, is not going to convert sloppy and/or right-wing reporters

into paragons of radical, painstakingly accurate journalism; but it will sow a seed of doubt that will make them a bit more careful in the future about trade-union stories, and it should also worry the editor, who would not want to be accused of carrying incorrect or biased pieces.

Sometimes things will go wrong no matter what you do and despite the journalists' best intentions.

> In 1978, London dockers held a press conference to protest against the proposed closure of the Royal London docks. During the course of the press conference, the docks officer of the TGWU said that to go on unofficial strike 'would be industrial suicide'. The man's name was Peter Shea. Also speaking at the press conference was Brian Nicholson, chairman of the Joint Dock Union's Committee. He took a much more militant line suggesting that a national dock strike might have to be called.
>
> Shea and Nicholson thus took almost opposite points of view. Their identities were clear to the reporters there.
>
> Yet, on *News at Ten* that night, in the middle of reading a piece on the docks story, the newscaster said: 'Dockers' leader, Mr Brian Nicholson, said it would be industrial suicide to go on strike over the issue.' Militant dockers fell off their chairs hearing their main rank-and-file leader quoted as uttering such a statement. ITN had got it wrong because of a mix-up *after* the reporter had handed in the piece and gone out on another job. An ITN scriptwriter had written the introduction to the film report and mixed up the two men.

The point is that, despite your best endeavours and despite using every trick in this book, things will still go wrong. What you must do is not simply shrug your shoulders and put it down to the evil machinations of the capitalist media. **You must complain.**

There are different ways of complaining and differing responses to a complaint. If you fail to get satisfaction, there are even ways of taking a complaint beyond the newsroom, programme, newspaper or broadcasting station.

Get the complaint right

Absolute accuracy is crucial when making a complaint. You must be able to pinpoint the facts that are wrong. This is a particular problem with television and radio, when you can't go back to check the words. If you hear or see something that is inaccurate in a programme, write it down at once. Trying to remember the offending words an hour later is virtually impossible.

Don't be obsessed with minor inaccuracies in figures or an incorrect use of terminology – for example, if a report says that 400 men went on strike when the total is actually 437. Nor is it really worth getting worked up if a reporter calls a regional secretary a divisional organiser. A friendly letter of correction is the way to deal with that problem.

Journalists are used to accusations of bias. They don't like being told unemotionally that they got something badly wrong. **Don't mix up a charge of political bias with a charge of inaccuracy. Keep the two separate and place most emphasis on the inaccuracy.**

Register it quickly

The quicker you are with your telephone-call about an offending item, the more impressed will the newsroom be that there is something seriously wrong. Ask to speak to the editor or producer, don't be put off by secretaries, insist that you have an important complaint and, when you get through, explain yourself firmly but politely.

Whatever the offence (but see **Libel,** below), the guilty party should be able to put it right by one of the following:

■ publishing a full retraction
■ putting it right 'in passing'
■ promising a better article in the future
■ promising to print a letter of complaint
■ saying that a letter will be considered for publication.

No editorial executive likes to admit to the public that he or she has got things wrong, so he/she will try to get you to accept something low down on this list. You, on the other hand, will try to get the highest item on the list you can. It is fairly rare for a newspaper to publish a full retraction except under legal pressure. But if the programme or article *was* in the wrong, the editor should be pressed to do an item in the next issue or programme which will get in the correction.

Don't expect to see something written saying: 'The *Daily News* would like to apologise to the General Mechanics Union for describing as unofficial the strike at Browns. It is in fact an official strike.' What will be written the next day will be: 'It has now been made clear that the strike at Browns reported yesterday to be unofficial is in fact an official strike and has the full backing of the General Mechanics Union.'

If you complain that a feature article about some issue has ignored the trade-union position and given a one-sided picture, the editor may find it difficult to run a story the next day, as it is not a developing news situation; but he or she will perhaps offer to send along a reporter in the near future to do a feature about the union's work.

The very least you want to extract from the editor is a promise to print a letter.

Libel

People who get written about unfairly in a newspaper often think they have been libelled. They are usually wrong. Journalists are careful about libel and any piece that a journalist or editor feels unsure about is usually read by a lawyer before it is published. National newspapers and the BBC have lawyers on their staff who do nothing else but check material for possible libel.

Libel covers all written and broadcast work. **Slander** is saying something defamatory about a person.

Libel is notoriously difficult to define. The three best-known legal definitions are:

■ a statement concerning any person which exposes him to hatred, ridicule or contempt or which causes him to be shunned or avoided or which has a tendency to injure him in his office, profession or trade

■ a false statement about a man to his discredit

■ would the words tend to lower the plaintiff in the estimation of right-thinking members of society generally?

But libel law is very much based on past cases and tends to get made up by judges and juries as they go along.

A libel does not have to appear in a newspaper. A letter or a report sent to one other person can be libellous. **Institutions (such as unions or firms) cannot be libelled, only individuals. However, if you say of a small firm that it has been involved in illegal or corrupt practices, it may be possible for the directors to sue, as the innuendo would be that they were responsible.**

Persons who hold some office – shop stewards, councillors, pressure-group chairpersons – are expected to be able to face harsh criticisms of their performance in that office. A newspaper can even describe you as a ringleader or a politically motivated militant or extremist and still be within the law. But to call a member of the Labour Party a Trotskyist or a Communist, for example, would be defamatory: membership of parties that put up candidates in opposition to Labour Party candidates (as does the CPGB, SWP, or IMG) is prohibited under Labour Party rules and the newspaper would, in effect, be accusing the person of lying. Any suggestion or allegation of financial impropriety is also usually defamatory.

A lawyer or a friendly journalist can advise on whether or not something is libellous. But libel law is a highly specialised branch of the law and, if you are to take the case further, you may have to engage specialist lawyers. At the end of the day both judges and juries are notoriously fickle on libel cases; and if you lose the case you will almost certainly have to pay the opposition's costs as well as your own.

If you feel you have been libelled, you should try and get the union to pay for the initial consultation with the solicitor. Quite often a sharp letter from a solicitor will produce a retraction: newspapers also know what a lottery libel actions are, and will sometimes settle for an apology at an early stage, even if they feel they have a case, because the judge or the jury might go the wrong way when it comes to court.

Be very careful about rushing into a libel suit on your own. It will almost certainly be costly and it can go horribly wrong.

The Press Council

The Press Council was set up in 1953, despite strenuous opposition from proprietors, to act as a kind of ethical watchdog on written journalism (it does not cover broadcasting) and as a body to adjudicate on complaints from the public about individual stories. It is not very highly respected amongst journalists, but no one likes to be taken to the Press Council and to have to defend a story. It remains a limited, if time-consuming, way of complaining about bad stories. The people who sit on it are all drawn from the establishment, with the exception of four NUJ representatives.

The Press Council has published its own guidance note on how to present a complaint. It runs as follows:

Guidance on procedure for complainants
It is open to any member of the public to initiate a case against a newspaper for breach of the unwritten ethical code of newspaper practice, whether it is due to publication or non-publication of statements or the conduct of press representatives. The procedure is simple.

Initially the aggrieved person may complain to the editor of the newspaper concerned. Most people appreciate, particularly in the case of inaccuracy, that this is a good way of seeking the prompt publication of a correction. Alternatively if a complainant chooses to send full particulars of the complaint by letter to the Director of the Press Council he will forward it to the editor, without commenting on the merits of the matter, so that he has the opportunity of dealing with the matter direct and taking any action he thinks fit. The Secretary (of the Press Council) will acknowledge receipt of the complainant's complaint.

If the complainant is not satisfied with the response to his representations (and this includes not receiving a reply within what he considers a reasonable time) and wishes to seek an adjudication by the Press Council, his next step is to send to the Director of the Press Council at No. 1 Salisbury Square, London EC4Y 8AE:

a. A statement of complaint;

b. Copies of all letters sent to the editor;

c. All letters received from the editor or from those acting on his behalf;

d. The page of the newspaper containing the matter complained of;

e. Names and addresses of witnesses if this is applicable; and

f. Any other evidence, including signed statements, if appropriate, which may support the complaint.

From this point the Press Council pursues its own investigations. A dossier of all the available evidence is compiled for careful sifting by the Complaints Committee which may also call for oral evidence.

Where the Council adjudicates, its decision is communicated to the parties and in all but exceptional cases a statement of the complaint and the adjudication on it is issued to the Press for publication.

It must be remembered that the Press Council is an ethical body and does not seek to supersede or supplement the administration of legal justice.

All documents submitted in presentation of a case will be retained by the Council in its Case Records and submission will be accounted acceptance of this rule.

Delays in the presentation of complaints sometimes seriously interfere with investigation by the Press Council and make unreasonable demands upon editors and journalists who wish to consult documents or obtain the evidence of witnesses. The Council therefore is concerned to seek the cooperation of the public in the prompt presentation of complaints and has decided that where there is unreasonable delay in submission it may decline to entertain complaints.

Similarly, the Council seeks to minimise delays in the response of newspaper editors and has authorised the Director, in appropriate cases, to fix time-limits for production of replies, in default of which the Council may proceed to deal with the complaints.

It is important, in cases involving disputed interviews, that editors or affected journalists shall provide the Council with notes taken at the time.

As you can see from the Press Council's own note of guidance, complaining is a long process and will require effort and commitment on your part.

Every reporter in the world has been told angrily some time or other, by someone or other, 'I'm going to take you to the Press Council over this.' It is a hollow threat. In 1976, out of the millions of newspaper stories that appeared, the Press Council received precisely 428 complaints. Of those, only 34 were upheld.

Thirty-four complaints upheld out of a year's-worth of newspaper and magazine stories! Either the press is well-nigh perfect, or no one in its readership can be bothered to complain, or the absorptive and delaying tactics of the Press Council – and, in many cases, very reactionary adjudications – mean that few people are ready to take it seriously.

Whether your complaint is rejected or upheld, the result and the adjudication will be published in the paper which was complained about. However, Press Council adjudications are never given the same prominence as the story that caused the complaint. They are normally tucked away at the bottom of one of the less well-read news pages. Some editors and most journalists openly profess their indifference to Press Council adjudications.

As it is, complaining to the Press Council is hardly worth the effort.

Complaints about broadcasting

In order to head off calls for a Broadcasting Council, which would operate in a similar way to the Press Council, both the BBC and the IBA have set up their own complaints committees. Neither is independent. The members are appointed by the BBC or the IBA and, although the committee members are doubtless men of personal integrity – usually superannuated judges – it is a standing reproach to the broadcasting corporations that there is no wholly independent complaints procedure. These complaints committees are not worth bothering with. **You should complain to and put pressure directly on the broadcasters.**

As soon as you see something in a programme or hear something on the radio that you know to be wrong, or consider to be unfair, telephone the studio or station and make the complaint. You should try and speak to the producer or editor. During the transmission of a live programme or news bulletin there are always journalists sitting around the newsroom or production office watching it go out. When you phone up, simply say 'Newsdesk, please' in an authoritative manner and you will be put through. Quickly say who you are and what your complaint is.

If it is about a serious error and you telephone straight away, there will be a fair chance that they will correct the mistake before the end of the bulletin or programme. If the complaint is about bias, or distortion, there is little point in having a long argument. Say who you are, make the complaint and tell him you will be writing in. Sometimes you will get diverted to a duty officer (that's the title in the BBC, but all television companies employ someone to sponge up viewers' telephone complaints), and you should make your complaint to him. It will get written down and a day or two later will work its way to the offending department.

Having made the immediate complaint by telephone, make sure you **follow it up with a letter.** Write to the top – the Director-General of the BBC or the Chairman of the Independent Broadcasting Authority – and send a copy to the editor or producer of the programme concerned.

Identify the programme or bulletin, the presenter or reporter and the subject, and then spell out unemotionally the aspect you thought was wrong or unfair. It is worth asking for a transcript of the interview or news item. This shows you mean business; often the request itself is enough to get things put right because the broadcasting management know that you are serious. If possible, type the letter; and, if possible, use union notepaper. Don't over-worry about this: a hand-written complaint will still be taken up.

Here is a complaint written to the BBC about a particular

news item. It is written from Hackney Community Relations Council, but its tone and style are a model for complaints about trade-union or political television-news coverage.

On Sunday, 16 October 1977, a demonstration and multi-cultural festival were held in London's East End. The demonstration had several objectives, one of which was to protest against the continuation of violent assaults on immigrants and their families living in the area. The demonstration, which incorporated a steel band, a jazz band and a pop group, proceeded from Shoreditch Park via Brick Lane to Victoria Park where the multi-cultural festival took place.

In the 5.35 p.m. News bulletin that day the BBC described the demonstration as being 'provocative', stated that it had been organised by the 'Socialist Workers Party' and there was no mention of the multi-cultural festival.

Apparently, following telephone calls from persons who had taken part in the day's events, the later bulletins dropped all references to the 'Socialist Workers Party' but otherwise they remained the same.

Our complaint rests on four grounds.

1. The BBC failed to take reasonable steps to ensure that they broadcasted accurate information about the day's events, or they were grossly negligent in ensuring that accurate information was used in the News bulletins.

2. The use of the word 'provocative' was unjustified and constitutes a breach of the duty cast upon the BBC to present news in a fair and proper context.

3. By failing to make any reference to the multi-cultural festival, the BBC presented a distorted view both of the actuality of the day's events and of one of the key themes underlying the whole venture.

4. A written apology in a letter does not constitute adequate redress for our complaint.

Hackney CRC failed with their complaint. Although CRC officers visited the BBC and persisted with the complaint over several months, the BBC still refused to broadcast a retraction or apology. However, an internal inquiry was held. The journalists responsible for the errror would, in the future, be forced to pay more attention to political attributions – if only to avoid the internal bureaucratic problems that a well-presented complaint will cause.

If you can, get an MP or senior local councillor or a senior trade-union official to make the complaint on your behalf. The broadcasters are nervous of politicians – the BBC, because MPs have to approve licence-fee increases, and the IBA because the government appoints its members, who then determine the allocation of radio and television franchises in commercial broadcasting.

Better still, get an MP to raise the matter in the House of Commons. Officially, the answer will be that editorial and policy matters are in the hands of the broadcasters; but neither the BBC nor any other television or radio company relish criticism in parliament, especially if it is well-founded. If the MP gets the timing right, he could even broadcast the complaint to the nation!

Other methods of complaint

Complain via the NUJ

The NUJ has a Code of Conduct which is part of the union rule-book. Only an NUJ member can complain under rule about the writings or actions of another NUJ member. But the Code of Conduct is useful as an example of the ethical standards against which journalism as it is practised can be judged.

NUJ Code of Conduct
1. A journalist has a duty to maintain the highest professional and ethical standards.

2. A journalist shall at all times defend the principle of the freedom of the press and other media in relation to the collection of information and the expression of comment and criticism. He/she shall strive to eliminate distortion, news suppression and censorship.

3. A journalist shall strive to ensure that the information he/she disseminates is fair and accurate, avoid the expression of comment and conjecture as established fact and falsification by distortion, selection or misrepresentation.

4. A journalist shall rectify promptly any harmful inaccuracies, ensure that corrections and apologies receive due prominence and afford the right of reply to persons criticised when the issue is of sufficient importance.

5. A journalist shall obtain information, photographs and illustrations only by straightforward means. The use of other means can be justified only by over-riding con-

siderations of public interest. The journalist is entitled to exercise a personal conscientious objection to the use of such means.

6. Subject to justification of over-riding considerations of the public interest, a journalist shall do nothing which entails the intrusion into private grief and distress.

7. A journalist shall protect confidential sources of information.

8. A journalist shall not accept bribes nor shall he/she allow other inducements to influence the performance of his/her professional duties.

9. A journalist shall not lend himself/herself to the distortion or suppression of the truth because of advertising or other considerations.

10. A journalist shall not originate or process material which encourages discrimination on grounds of race, colour, creed, gender or sexual orientation.

11. A journalist shall not take private advantage of information gained in the course of his/her duties, before the information is public knowledge.

12. A journalist shall not by way of statement, voice or appearance endorse by advertisement any commercial product or service save for the promotion of his/her own work or of the medium by which he/she is employed.

It is not the NUJ's job to act as an ethical policeman on behalf of other trade unionists who feel aggrieved by newspaper reports. But it is perfectly reasonable to contact the FoC of a newspaper or broadcasting station if you feel there is persistent error or bias in coverage. On a union-to-union basis it is possible to pass a motion at your branch and send it to the NUJ branch or chapel. Better still ask to go along to a chapel or branch meeting and explain your concern.

Compile a dossier

It is very easy to get steamed up about one isolated front-page story, or even just a single headline. Journalists are used to these complaints and, even when they are in the wrong, tend to shrug off the complaint by saying (and even believing) that it was a one-off error or a chance mistake. **That line of defence is not open to them if a long list of stories, feature articles, unfair intros, sensational headlines and unbalanced quotes is compiled and presented.**

A branch or trades-council sub-committee can be elected to do the work. It has to cut and keep all industrial stories from a paper over a period of time (for example, three months) and analyse them carefully, pointing out errors and distortions. It is painstaking work and needs a degree of commitment and enthusiasm from those involved. You should be careful to avoid overdoing your search for bias and trying to justify a complaint on spurious grounds: 'When in doubt, leave it out' is an old journalistic saying and it applies to complaints about journalism as much as to the craft itself.

The dossier can be compiled as a report to the branch or trades council, and then sent out with a press release to the other local media, to some of the national dailies (for example, the *Guardian* and *Morning Star*) and to the journalists' trade paper, the *UK Press Gazette* (Cliffords Inn, Fetter Lane, London EC4) as well as to the NUJ itself.

Picket and petition

At the end of the day, trade unions have always relied on direct action to make an effective protest. This can be applied to press coverage as to anything else. If there is genuine concern amongst members about a particular paper's reporting, then a public and dramatic way of bringing public pressure to bear is to organise a picket to demonstrate outside the office.

The purpose of the picket should be *to give information* – not to try and stop people from going to work, but to explain to workers on the paper and to the public the concern felt about unfair coverage. There will have to be genuine and deep-felt concern and you will want to muster as many people as possible with all the usual paraphernalia of picketing – placards, leaflets and so on.

In 1979, the editor of the *Hornsey Journal* wrote a front-page article attacking low-pay strikes. He accused council workers in Haringey of organising a 'carefully orchestrated exercise in trade-union power'. Angry trade unionists contacted the NUJ chapel on the *Hornsey Journal*, told them they were going to demonstrate outside the newspaper's office and asked for the journalists' support in demanding a right of reply. They won. The next issue carried both a statement from the strikers and a letter from the journalists dissociating themselves from the editor's article.

In 1976, the management at Radio Trent agreed to drop a phone-in programme with a local National Front leader when anti-fascists made clear that a major demonstration would be held outside the station if it went ahead.

In 1977, feminists occupied the London *Evening News* to protest at a story about lesbian mothers being artificially insemi-
nated. Their objection was not to the story itself but to the
sensational way it had been displayed in the paper and to the
technique used in obtaining the story. The editor agreed to give
them space for an article outlining their objections.

You can also use the traditional petition to complain about
unfair reporting. The more signatures the better. In any large
workplace it should be possible over a few days to get people to
sign. When you send the petition to the editor concerned, also
send it to other media with a covering press release explaining
the reasons behind it.

Table a motion

Workers should use to the maximum the internal trade-
union mechanisms for raising issues – in this case, specific and
general complaints about media coverage. Motions can be tabled
and debated at branches, trades council, regional councils of the
TUC, district, divisional and regional union bodies and at the
annual conferences of unions or the TUC.

**It is better to concentrate on individual papers or pro-
grammes.** A generalised motion condemning the media, like this
one tabled by ASLEF at the 1976 TUC Congress –

Congress does not condone the anarchistic interference by
the news media in trade-union elections, and calls on the
Government to initiate more democratic control over these
agencies.

– does not help persuade journalists – let alone editors and
proprietors – that they should mend their ways. During that
same Congress, both Alf Allen and Hugh Scanlon made some
sharp remarks in general terms (Allen had referred to the
'vultures of the press'), and at the end of the week the then General
Secretary of the NUJ, Ken Morgan, gently remonstrated with
the press critics; but he also went on to make an important point
about how to criticise and complain about press coverage:

'I want to urge that when responding as a movement to
attacks from the press we respond by defending ourselves
with an accurate sniper's rifle which can be aligned on the
right target, rather than by blasting off a great blunderbuss
which scatters everyone in sight.'

If the newspapers or television or radio programmes are not named, journalists will say to themselves, 'Well, it's not me or my paper they are complaining about.'

Even the tabling of a motion can have an impact if you distribute a press release announcing that the motion has been tabled and adding some comments on the reason for tabling it.

13.

Press officers and media training

The role of the press officer / equipping a regional press office / media training within unions

The role of the press officer

It is often assumed that a secretary or chairperson can double as a press officer. In fact, being a *good* press officer is an important job in itself in a trade-union or community-group structure.

His or her job should be to:

■ keep cuttings of all relevant stories

■ monitor radio and television for mention of the union or workplace or organisation

■ issue press releases

■ devise briefings and campaigns that will use the media

■ organise news conferences

■ think of feature or investigative stories and 'sell' the ideas to newspapers, magazines and radio and television programmes

■ invite local NUJ officers and/or editors to address union meetings

■ press NUJ branches and chapels to have union speakers

■ organise complaints when coverage is wrong or unfair

■ persuade colleagues about the necessity of using the media.

It is a job which, if it is to be done seriously and well, needs time and careful attention. The press officer will need to show considerable initiative. He or she must be someone who enjoys the confidence of the body on whose behalf he or she makes comments. The press officer must be able to answer inquiries or make statements, if necessary under the guise of being a spokesperson (see page 120), without incurring anyone's wrath later on.

One of the first tasks is to make a **systematic list of local media** (see the example list for South Birmingham).

Table 1: Media list for South Birmingham

	telephone
News Editor/Industrial Correspondent Birmingham *Evening Mail* Colmore Circus, Birmingham 4	021 236 3366
Solihull District Office Birmingham *Evening Mail* 25–27 High Street Solihull	021 705 3545 704 9956
News Editor/Industrial Correspondent *Birmingham Post* Colmore Circus, Birmingham 4	021 236 3366
News Editor *Sunday Mercury* Colmore Circus, Birmingham 4	021 236 3366
Caters (the Birmingham Freelance News Agency) 184 Corporation Street, Birmingham 4	021 236 9001
News Editor *Solihull News* (weekly newspaper covering Solihull and South Birmingham) 52 Drury Lane, Solihull	021 705 8211
Newsdesk *Midlands Today* BBC TV Pebble Mill Road Birmingham B5 7SO	021 472 5353
Newsdesk *ATV Today* ATV Centre Birmingham B1 2JP	021 643 9898

News Editor
BBC Radio Birmingham
Pebble Mill Road
Birmingham B5 7SO   021 472 5141

News Editor
BRMB (Birmingham's commercial radio station)
PO Box 555
Aston Road North
Birmingham BS4 BX   021 359 4481

Birmingham Broadside
(monthly magazine combining left-wing journalism
with a list of current films, plays, etc.)
81 Grove Lane
Birmingham B21   021 554 3295

All the national newspapers and the Press Association have a staff journalist based in Birmingham. Some work from offices in the city centre, others work from home. To get the names, addresses and telephone-numbers of national-newspaper staff reporters working in the major provincial cities it is best to contact their head offices in London or to ask the local freelance news agency.

It would be impractical to try to keep in similarly systematic contact with the national media, particularly with routine news (although, if secretarial facilities are available, it may be worth sending material to the Fleet Street papers). If the story is a big enough one in news terms, the local freelances or, in some cases, journalists on the local paper, will sell it to the London papers. The same is broadly true of the BBC local radio and regional television stations: they are expected to tell the national BBC Radio and Television newsrooms if anything of national news interest happens in their area.

The press officer should concentrate on the *local* media, and adopt a professional approach. Good press relations are founded on good systems – random letters and phone-calls are no substitute.

Equipping a regional press office

Large trade unions with well-staffed regional offices still do not pay enough attention to the media. As well as providing good media training, any big trade-union region should also have some efficient system for recording what mention of union activities there is in the regional press, television and radio. All the evening papers in the region should be subscribed to and it should be someone's responsibility to read each paper and cut out relevant stories.

A radio cassette recorder is essential for recording broadcast interviews and phone-ins (these can now be bought quite cheaply). If you ever have a complaint to make, or want to take action over libel, it will be imperative that you have your own recording of exactly what was broadcast. Also, if you are involved in a news conference or a radio interview, it can be useful to record the questions and answers; reporters will then know that, if any unfair editing takes place, you will have a record of what was originally said.

Television videotape recorders are now coming down in price. Along with a television set, one of these is another essential piece of equipment for any large trade-union regional office wanting to take media relations seriously. If you have a recording of a television programme, you are in a much stronger position to vet it for fairness. A video recorder is also a vital tool for officials or shop stewards who appear live in studio discussions or interviews and want to examine and improve their performance.

TV video recorders are not only useful for media purposes. They can also be used to great effect for training and education purposes.

Some regional offices have telex machines. These can be used to send press releases or statements direct to most evening and morning newspapers, and to television and radio stations.

Media training within unions

Unions run courses on all sorts of subjects – from safety and employers' accounts, to industrial tribunals and negotiating tactics. But they give almost no attention to the media, although newspapers and television play such a vital part in deciding how workers approach key union issues.

The TUC runs an excellent week-long course – but that can only cater for three dozen full-time officials per year. The AUEW trains the members of its parliamentary panel on how to be interviewed by newspaper journalists and how to appear on television – but does not lay on similar courses for its union leaders. NUPE is beginning to include media training in some of its courses, but still at a rudimentary level – and this despite the fantastic importance of the media in determining public response to some of the public-sector disputes in which NUPE has been engaged since the early 1970s. Few other unions make any effort. Their media image, the effectiveness with which their local officers (lay or full-time) present the members' case in the media – this is regarded with indifference, as a matter of luck. If you get bad coverage, you just blame it on the wicked capitalist press.

The fault lies just as much in the unions' ignorance of how the press can be used. Unions should be pressed to include proper media training in the courses they offer – and that means two or three *days*, not just a quick three-hour lecture in the middle of some general introductory course.

At regional level, unions should provide **weekend schools** on using the media. Many journalists working on provincial evening newspapers, television and radio would be willing to help. Most polytechnics now have some videotape equipment which would allow a rudimentary training course on television techniques. For radio training, all that is needed is a cassette recorder, a microphone and a radio journalist willing to do interviews and comment on them afterwards.

At national level, unions should be pressed to **hire more journalists as press officers, as journal editors and as general advisers** on handling the media. Such people could then educate right through the ranks of the unions on the professional use of the media.

Unions should be continually challenging the ownership, control and purpose of the media. We need a press that is more free, and more responsive to the needs of all the community.

14.

Directory of press, radio and television

All circulation figures are taken from the Audit Bureau of Circulation January–June 1978.

National media

Daily newspapers

Daily Express
Fleet Street
London EC4
tel: 01-353 8000
circulation: 2,466,000 copies

Daily Mail
New Carmelite House
London EC4
tel: 01-353 6000
1,988,000

Daily Mirror
Holborn Circus
London EC1
tel: 01-353 0246
3,914,000

Daily Star
27 Tudor Street
London EC4
tel: 01-583 9199
1,011,116

Daily Telegraph
Fleet Street
London EC4
tel: 01-353 4242
1,357,000

Financial Times
Bracken House
Cannon Street
London EC4
tel: 01-248 8000
179,000

Guardian
119 Farringdon Road
London EC1
tel: 01-278 2332
275,000

Morning Star
75 Farringdon Road
London EC1
tel: 01-405 9242
22,000 (another 14,000 sold abroad)

Newsline
21b Old Town
Clapham
London SW4
tel: 01-720 2000
(no circulation figure available)

Sun
30 Bouverie Street
London EC4
tel: 01-353 3030
4,017,000

The Times
New Printing House Square
Grays Inn Road
London WC1
tel: 01-837 1234
292,714

Sunday newspapers

News of the World
30 Bouverie Street
London EC4
tel: 01-353 3030

circulation: 4,925,000 copies

Observer
8 St Andrews Hill
London EC4
tel: 01-236 0202

678,098

Sunday Express
Fleet Street
London EC4
tel: 01-353 8000

3,239,000

Sunday Mirror
Holborn Circus
London EC1
tel: 01-353 0246

3,858,000

Sunday People
Holborn Circus
London EC1
tel: 01-353 0246

3,889,000

Sunday Telegraph
Fleet Street
London EC4
tel: 01-353 4242

842,590

Sunday Times
New Printing House Square
Grays Inn Road
London WC1
tel: 01-837 1234

1,402,000

London editorial offices of regional chains

Associated Newspapers
Northcliffe House West
London EC4
tel: 01-353 6000

Thomson Regional Newspapers
Greater London House
Hampstead Road
London NW1
tel: 01-387 2800

United Newspapers
23–27 Tudor Street
London EC4
tel: 01-583 9199

Westminster Press
8–16 Great New Street
London EC4
tel: 01-353 1030

News agencies

Press Association
Fleet Street
London EC4
tel: 01-353 7440

Universal News Service
Communications House
Gough Square
London EC4
tel: 01-353 5200

Picture agency

Report
411 Oxford Street
London W1
tel: 01-493 7737

Broadcasting newsrooms

BBC Television News
Television Centre
Wood Lane
London W12
tel: 01-743 8000
(extension 3941)

BBC Television Current Affairs
Lime Grove
London W12
tel: 01-743 8000

BBC Radio News and Current
Affairs
Broadcasting House
Portland Place
London W1
tel: 01-580 4468
(extension 2036/7)

Independent Radio News
Gough Square
London EC4
tel: 01-353 1010

Regional media

London

Newspapers

Evening News
New Carmelite House
London EC4
tel: 01-353 6000

circulation: 529,838 copies

Evening Standard
47 Shoe Lane
London EC4
tel: 01-353 8000

361,958

Broadcasting

Thames Television
306–316 Euston Road
London NW1
tel: 01-387 9494

London Weekend Television
Kent House
Upper Ground
London SE1
tel: 01–261 3434

BBC Radio London
35a Marylebone High Street
London W1
tel: 01-486 7611

LBC
Gough Square
London EC4
tel: 01-353 1010

Capital Radio
Euston Tower
London NW1
tel: 01-388 1288

Home counties and South-East

Newspapers

Basildon (Southend)
Evening Echo
Chester Hall Lane
Basildon
Essex
tel: 0268 22792

circulation: 64,054 copies

Brighton
Evening Argus
89 North Road
Brighton
tel: 0273 606799

106,275

Chatham
Kent Evening Post
395 High Street
Chatham
Kent
tel: 0634 42556

41,687

Guildford
Surrey Daily Advertiser
Martyr Road
Guildford
Surrey
tel: 0483 71234

(circulation figure not available)

Hemel Hempstead (also Watford
and Luton)
Evening Post-Echo
Mark Road
Hemel Hempstead
Herts
tel: 0442 42277

86,661

Reading
Evening Post
Tessa Road
Reading
Berkshire
tel: 0734 55833

49,039

Slough
Evening Mail
1 Stoke Road
Slough
Bucks
tel: 75 32041

31,749

Radio

BBC Radio Brighton
Marlborough Place
Brighton
Sussex
tel: 0273 680231

BBC Radio Medway
30 High Street
Chatham
Kent
tel: 0634 46284

Radio 210 (Reading)
Thames Valley Broadcasting
PO Box 210
Reading
Berkshire
tel: 0734 413131

South

Newspapers

Bournemouth
Evening Echo
Richmond Hill
Bournemouth
tel: 0202 24601

circulation: 65,007 copies

Portsmouth
The News
The News Centre
Hilsea
Portsmouth
tel: 0705 64488

106,013

Southampton
Southern Evening Echo
Above Bar
Southampton
tel: 0703 34134

101,027

Weymouth
Dorset Evening Echo
57 St Thomas Street
Weymouth
Dorset
tel: 03057 4804

24,441

Radio

Radio Victory
PO Box 257
Portsmouth
tel: 0705 27799

BBC Radio Solent
(Southampton)
South Western House
Canute Road
Southampton
tel: 0703 31311

Television

Southern Television
Northam
Southampton
tel: 0703 28582

BBC South
South Western House
Canute Road
Southampton
tel: 0703 26201

South-West

Newspapers

Exeter
Express and Echo
160 Sidwell Street
Exeter
tel: 0392 73051

circulation: 37,782 copies

Plymouth
Western Morning News (morning)
Leicester Harmsworth House
Plymouth
tel: 0752 266626

63,471

Western Evening Herald (evening)
as above
63,974

Sunday Independent (Sunday)
Burrington Way
Honicknowle
Plymouth
tel: 0752 777151

62,160

Torquay
Herald Express
23 Fleet Street
Torquay
tel: 0803 22261

25,788

Radio

Plymouth Sound
Earls Acre
Alma Road
Plymouth
tel: 0752 27272

Television

Westward Television
Derry's Cross
Plymouth
tel: 0752 69311

BBC South West
Seymour Road
Mannamead
Plymouth
tel: 0752 62283

West

Newspapers

Bath
Bath and West Evening Chronicle
33–34 Westgate Street
Bath
tel: 0225 5871

circulation: 32,699 copies

Bristol
Western Daily Press (morning)
Temple Way
Bristol
tel: 0272 20080

79,073

Bristol Evening Post
as above
137,702

Gloucester
The Citizen
St John's Lane
Gloucester
tel: 0452 24442

36,695

Swindon
Evening Advertiser
Newspaper House
Swindon
Wiltshire
tel: 0793 28144

37,290

Radio

BBC Radio Bristol
3 Tyndalls Park Road
Bristol
tel: 0272 311111

Television

HTV West
Television Centre
Bath Road
Bristol
tel: 0272 770271

BBC West
Broadcasting House
21–33b Whiteladies Road
Bristol
tel: 0272 32211

Midlands

Newspapers

Birmingham
Birmingham Post (morning)
28 Colmore Circus
Birmingham 4
tel: 021-236 3366

circulation: 45,080 copies

Evening Mail (evening)
as above

341,259

Sunday Mercury (Sunday)
as above

200,106

Burton
Burton Daily Mail
65–68 High Street
Burton on Trent
DE14 1LE
tel: 0283 43311

21,425

Cheltenham
Gloucestershire Echo
1 Clarence Parade
Cheltenham
tel: 0242 26261

31,372

Coventry
Coventry Evening Telegraph
Corporation Street
Coventry
0203 25588

112,196

Derby
Derby Evening Telegraph
Northcliffe House
Albert Street,
Derby
tel: 0332 42400

88,604

Hereford
Evening News
Berrow's House
Hereford
tel: 0432 4413

37,893

Kettering
*Northamptonshire Evening
Telegraph*
Northfield Avenue
Kettering
tel: 0536 81111

47,175

Leamington
*Leamington and District Morning
News*
PO Box 45
Tachbrook Road
Leamington Spa
Warwickshire
tel: 0926 21122

10,457

Leicester
Leicester Mercury
St George Street
Leicester
tel: 0533 20831

167,000

Northampton
Chronicle and Echo
Upper Mounts
Northampton
tel: 0604 21122

48,148

Nottingham
Nottingham Evening Post*
Forman Street
Nottingham
tel: 0602 45521

144,373

Nuneaton
Nuneaton Evening Tribune
Watling House
Whitacre Road
Nuneaton
tel: 0682 382251

17,817

Oxford
Oxford Mail
Osney Mead
Oxford
tel: 0865 44988

40,035

Sandwell (West Bromwich)
Sandwell Evening Mail
402 High Street
West Bromwich
Staffs
tel: 021-553 7221
(circulation combined with
Evening Mail, Birmingham)

Stoke-on-Trent
Evening Sentinel
Foundry Street
Hanley
Stoke-on-Trent
tel: 0782 29511

124,738

Telford (Shrewsbury)
Shropshire Star
Ketley
Telford
Shropshire
tel: 0952 44377

81,678

*The *Nottingham Evening Post* may be
proscribed following the NUJ strike of
78–79. Management are refusing to
re-instate 27 journalists.

Wolverhampton
Express and Star
Queen Street
Wolverhampton
tel: 0902 22351

247,839

Worcester
Evening News
Berrow's House
Worcester
tel: 0905 423434

37,893

Radio

BRMB (Birmingham)
Radio House
PO Box 555
Birmingham 6
tel: 021 359 4481/9

BBC Radio Birmingham
Pebble Mill Road
Birmingham 5
tel: 021-472 5141

Beacon Radio (Wolverhampton)
PO Box 303
Wolverhampton
tel: 0902 757211

BBC Radio Stoke
Conway House
Cheapside
Hanley
Stoke-on-Trent
Staffs
tel: 0782 24827

BBC Radio Leicester
Epic House
Charles Street
Leicester
tel: 0533 27113

BBC Radio Derby
56 St Helens Street
Derby
tel: 0332 361111

Radio Trent (Nottingham)
29–31 Castle Gate
Nottingham
tel: 0602 581731

BBC Radio Nottingham
York House
York Street
Nottingham
tel: 0602 47643

Television

ATV
ATV Centre
Birmingham 1
tel: 021-643 9898

BBC Midlands
Pebble Mill Road
Birmingham 5
tel: 021-472 5353

Manchester and the North-West

Manchester newsrooms of national newspapers

Daily Express
Great Ancoats Street
Manchester M60 4HB
tel: 061-236 2112

Daily Mail
Northcliffe House
Deansgate
Manchester M60 3BA
tel: 061-834 8600

Daily Mirror
22 Hardman Street
Deansgate
Manchester M60 3BA
tel: 061-832 3444

Daily Telegraph
Withy Grove
Manchester
tel: 061-834 1234

Guardian
164 Deansgate
Manchester M60 2RR
tel: 061-832 7200

Daily Star
Great Ancoats Street
Manchester M60 4HB
tel: 061-236 2112

Regional newspapers

Manchester
Manchester Evening News
164 Deansgate
Manchester M60 2RD
tel: 061-832 7200

Barrow
North-Western Evening Mail
Abbey Road
Barrow-in-Furness
tel: 0229 21835

circulation: 27,307 copies

Blackburn
Lancashire Evening Telegraph
Telegraph House
Blackburn
tel: 0254 55291

58,597

Blackpool
West Lancashire Evening Gazette
Victoria Street
Blackpool
tel: 0253 25231

64,288

Bolton
Evening News
Mealhouse Lane
Bolton
tel: 0204 22345

73,816

Burnley
Evening Star
St James Street
Burnley
tel: 0282 23161

21,425

Carlisle
Evening News and Star
Newspaper House
Dalston Road
Carlisle
tel: 0228 23488

28,099

Liverpool
Liverpool Daily Post (morning)
PO Box 48
Old Hall Street
Liverpool L69 3EB
tel: 051-227 2000

84,767

Liverpool Echo (evening)
as above

256,159

Oldham
Evening Chronicle
Union Street
Oldham
tel: 061-633 2121

43,968

Preston
Lancashire Evening Post
127 Fishergate
Preston
tel: 0772 54841

104,047

Radio

BBC Radio Blackburn
King Street
Blackburn
tel: 0254 62411

BBC Radio Carlisle
Hilltop Heights
London Road
Carlisle
tel: 0228 31661

Radio City (Liverpool)
PO Box 194
8–10 Stanley Street
Liverpool L69 1LD
tel: 051-227 5100

BBC Radio Merseyside
Commerce House
13/17 Sir Thomas Street
Liverpool L15 BS
tel: 051-236 3355

Piccadilly Radio (Manchester)
127/131 The Piazza
Manchester M1 4AW
tel: 061-236 9913

BBC Radio Manchester
New Broadcasting House
Oxford Road
Manchester
tel: 061-228 3434

Television

Granada
Granada TV Centre
Manchester M60 9EA
tel: 061-832 7211

Border Television (Cumbria and
Isle of Man)
Television Centre
Carlisle
tel: 0228 25101

BBC North-West
New Broadcasting House
Oxford Road
Manchester M60 1SJ
tel: 061-236 8444

North

Newspapers

Bradford
Telegraph and Argus
Hall Ings
Bradford
tel: 0274 29511

circulation: 105,684 copies

Doncaster
Doncaster Evening Post
North Bridge Road
Doncaster
tel: 0302 4001

29,632

Halifax
Evening Courier
King Cross Street
Halifax
tel: 0422 65711

38,783

Huddersfield
Huddersfield Daily Examiner
Ramsden Street
Huddersfield
tel: 0484 27201

48,002

Hull
Hull Daily Mail
84 Jameson Street
Hull
tel: 0482 27111

128,177

Leeds
Yorkshire Post (morning)
Wellington Street
Leeds
tel: 0532 32701
100,423
Evening Post (evening)
as above

184,377

Scarborough
Scarborough Evening News
Aberdeen Walk
Scarborough
tel: 0723 63631

18,849

Scunthorpe
Scunthorpe Evening Telegraph
Doncaster Road
Scunthorpe
tel: 0724 3421

(connected with *Grimsby Evening Telegraph*)

Sheffield
Morning Telegraph
York Street
Sheffield
tel: 0742 78585

41,834
The Star (evening)
as above

158,148

York
Yorkshire Evening Press
15 Coney Street
York
tel: 0904 53051

62,161

Radio

Pennine Radio (Bradford)
PO Box 235
Pennine House
Forster Square
Bradford
tel: 0274 31521

BBC Radio Humberside (Hull)
9 Chapel Street
Hull
tel: 0482 23232

BBC Radio Leeds
Merrion Centre
Leeds
tel: 0532 42131

Radio Hallam (Sheffield and
Rotherham)
PO Box 194
Hartshead
Sheffield
tel: 0742 71188

BBC Radio Sheffield
Ashdell Grove
60 Westbourne Road
Sheffield
tel: 0742 686185

Television

Yorkshire Television
Television Centre
Leeds
tel: 0532 38283

BBC North
Broadcasting Centre
Woodhouse Lane
Leeds
tel: 0532 41181/8

East Anglia and Lincolnshire

Newspapers

Cambridge
Cambridge Evening News
51 Newmarket Road
Cambridge
tel: 0223 58877
circulation: 51,556 copies

Colchester
Evening Gazette
Culver Street
Colchester
tel: 0206 5101
31,288

Grimsby
Grimsby Evening Telegraph
80 Cleethorpes Road
Grimsby
tel: 0472 59232
75,433

Ipswich
East Anglian Daily Times
(morning)
Lower Brook Street
Ipswich
tel: 0473 56777
42,222

Evening Star (evening)
as above
37,683

Lincoln
Lincolnshire Echo
St Benedict Square
Lincoln
tel: 0522 26101
39,598

Norwich
Eastern Daily Press (morning)
Prospect House
Rouen Road
Norwich
tel: 0603 28311
93,605

Eastern Evening News (evening)
as above
59,594

Peterborough
Peterborough Evening Telegraph
Oundle Road
Woodston
Peterborough
tel: 0733 68900
30,942

Radio

Radio Orwell
Electric House
Lloyds Avenue
Ipswich
tel: 0473 216971

Television

Anglia Television
Anglia House
Norwich
tel: 0603 28366

BBC East
St Catherine's Close
All Saints Green
Norwich
tel: 0603 28841

North-East

Newspapers

Darlington
Northern Echo (morning)
Priestgate
Darlington
tel: 0325 60177

circulation: 104,496 copies

Evening Despatch (evening)
as above
15,108

Hartlepool
Hartlepool Mail
West House
Clarence Road
Hartlepool
tel: 0429 4441
33,531

Middlesbrough
Evening Gazette
Gazette Buildings
Middlesbrough
tel: 0642 245401
97,952

Newcastle
The Journal (morning)
Thomson House
Groat Market
Newcastle upon Tyne
tel: 0632 27500
86,495

Evening Chronicle (evening)
as above
176,735

South Shields
Shields Gazette
Chapter Row
South Shields
tel: 0632 554661
34,485

Sunderland
Sunderland Echo
Pennywell Industrial Estate
Sunderland
Tyne and Wear
tel: 0783 243011
74,982

Radio

BBC Radio Cleveland
(Middlesbrough)
91/93 Linthorpe Road
Middlesbrough
Cleveland
tel: 0642 48491

Radio Tees (Stockport)
74 Dovecot Street
Stockton-on-Tees
Cleveland
tel: 0642 615111

Metro Radio (Newcastle)
Newcastle upon Tyne
NE99 1BB
tel: 0632 884121

BBC Radio Newcastle
Crestina House
Archbold Terrace
Newcastle upon Tyne
tel: 0632 814243

Television

Tyne Tees Television
The Television Centre
City Road
Newcastle upon Tyne
tel: 0632 610181

BBC North East
Broadcasting House
54 New Bridge Street
Newcastle upon Tyne
tel: 0632 20961

Scotland

Newspapers

Glasgow
Daily Record (morning)
Anderston Quay
Glasgow
tel: 041-248 7000
circulation: 721,645 copies

Sunday Mail (Sunday)
as above
770,759

Glasgow Herald (morning)
70 Mitchell Street
Glasgow
tel: 041-221 9200
116,180

Evening Times (evening)
as above
225,990

Edinburgh
The Scotsman (morning)
28 North Bridge
Edinburgh
tel: 031 225 2468
89,145

Evening News
as above
136,423

Aberdeen
Press and Journal (morning)
PO Box 43
Lang Stracht
Mastrick
Aberdeen
tel: 0224 690222
114,552

Evening Express (evening)
as above
77,365

Dundee*
Courier and Telegraph
Bank Street
Dundee
tel: 0382 23131
135,137

Evening Telegraph (evening)
as above
58,472

Sunday Post (Sunday)
Albert Square
Dundee
tel: 0382 23131
1,650,000

Greenock
Greenock Telegraph
2 Crawford Street
Greenock
tel: 0475 23301
24,681

Paisley
Paisley Daily Express
20 New Street
Paisley
tel: 041-887 7911
16,092

Radio

Radio Clyde (Glasgow)
Ranken House
Anderston Cross Centre
Glasgow
tel: 041-204 2555

*The three newspapers produced in
Dundee are owned by D.C. Thomson,
which has refused to recognise trade
unions since 1926. Many trade-union
members work as journalists and printers
there; regular campaigns are mounted to
try and persuade D.C. Thomson
management to recognise trade unions,
and during such campaigns the newspaper
offices are sometimes declared black.
Trade unions should contact D.C.
Thomson newspaper union officials before
sending in press releases etc.

BBC Radio Scotland
Broadcasting House
Queen Margaret Drive
Glasgow
tel: 041-339 8844

Radio Forth (Edinburgh)
Forth House
Forth Street
Edinburgh
tel: 031-556 9255

VHF radio stations

BBC Radio Aberdeen
Broadcasting House
Beechgrove Terrace
Aberdeen
tel: 0224 25233

BBC Radio Highland (Inverness)
7 Calduthel Road
Inverness
tel: 0463 22171

BBC Radio Orkney
6 Brighe Street
Wynd
Kirkwall
Orkney
tel: 0856 3939

BBC Radio Shetland
Lerwick
Shetland
tel: 0595 4747

Television

Scottish Television (STV)
Cowcaddens
Glasgow
tel: 041-332 9999

BBC TV Scotland:

Glasgow
Broadcasting House
Queen Margaret Drive
Glasgow
tel: 041-339 8844

Edinburgh
Broadcasting House
5 Queen Street
Edinburgh
tel: 031-225 3131

Aberdeen
Broadcasting House
Beechgrove Crescent
Aberdeen
tel: 0224 25233

Grampian Television
Queen's Cross
Aberdeen
tel: 0224 53553

Wales

Newspapers

Cardiff
Western Mail (morning)
Thomson House
Cardiff
tel: 0222 33022
circulation: 95,402 copies

South Wales Echo (evening)
as above
120,444

Newport
South Wales Argus
Cardiff Road
Newport
Gwent
tel: 0633 62241
54,864

Swansea
South Wales Evening Post
Adelaide Street
Swansea
tel: 0792 50841
69,620

Wrexham
Wrexham Evening Leader
Centenary Buildings
King Street
Wrexham
tel: 0978 55151
26,357

Radio

Swansea Sound
Victoria Road
Gowerton
Swansea
tel: 0792 893751

BBC Wales (Radio and
Television)
Broadcasting House
Llantrisant Road
Llandaff
Cardiff
tel: 0222 564888

Television

BBC TV Wales
see above

HTV Wales
Television Centre
Cardiff
tel: 0222 21021

Northern Ireland

Newspapers

Belfast
Belfast Telegraph (evening)
124–132 Royal Avenue
Belfast
tel: 0232 21242
circulation: 156,247 copies

Newsletter (morning)
51–59 Donegal Street
Belfast
tel: 0232 44441
60,463

Sunday News (Sunday)
as above
90,085

Irish News
113–117 Donegal Street
Belfast
tel: 0232 42614
49,163

Radio

Downtown Radio
Kiltonga Radio Centre
PO Box 293
Newtownards
Co Down
N. Ireland
tel: 0247 815211

BBC Radio Ulster
Broadcasting House
25–27 Ormeau Avenue
Belfast
tel: 0232 44400

Television

Ulster Television (UTV)
Havelock House
Ormeau Road
Belfast
tel: 0232 28122

BBC Northern Ireland
Broadcasting House
25–27 Ormeau Road
Belfast
tel: 0232 44400

Channel Islands

Newspapers

Guernsey
Guernsey Evening Press and Star
8 Smith Street
St Peter Port
Guernsey
tel: 0481 24661
circulation: 15,670 copies

Jersey
Jersey Evening Post
Five Oaks
St Saviour
Jersey
tel: 0534 73333
21,972

Television

Channel Television
Television Centre
St Helier
Jersey
tel: 0534 23451

Les Arcades
St Peter Port
Guernsey
tel: 0481 23451

Eire

Newspapers

Cork
Cork Examiner (morning)
95 Patrick Street
Cork
tel: Cork 26661
circulation: 66,438 copies

Cork Evening Echo (evening)
as above
40,831

Dublin
Irish Independent (morning)
90 Middle Abbey Street
Dublin
tel: 0001 746121
174,276

Evening Herald (evening)
as above
117,595

The Irish Press (morning)
Irish Press House
Dublin
tel: 0001 741871
93,598

Evening Press (evening)
as above
161,303

Irish Times (morning)
13 D'Olier Street
Dublin
tel: 0001 722022
66,242

Sunday Independent
see *Irish Independent*
276,217

The Sunday Press
see *The Irish Press*
384,521

Sunday World
18 Rathfarnham Road
Dublin
tel: 0001 978111
319,218

Radio and Television

RTE Cork
Union Quay
Cork
tel: Cork 25248

Radio Na Gaeltachta
Casla
Conamara
tel: Galway 2161

Radio Telefis Eireann
RTE
Donnybrook
Dublin 4
tel: 0001 693111

Weekly news magazines

The Economist
25 St James's Street
London SW1
tel: 01-930 5155

New Society
Kings Reach Tower
Stamford Street
London SE1
tel: 01-836 4736

New Statesman
10 Great Turnstile
London WC1
tel: 01-405 8471

Time Out
Tower House
Southampton Street
London WC2
tel: 01-836 4411

Left newspapers/ journals

Big Flame
217 Wavertree Road
Liverpool

Challenge
16 King Street
London WC2
tel: 01-836 2151

Comment
16 King Street
London WC2
tel: 01-836 2151

Cooperative News
418 Chester Road
Manchester
tel: 061-878 2991

Labour Monthly
134 Ballards Lane
London N3
tel: 01-346 5135

Labour Research
78 Blackfriars Road
London SE1
tel: 01-928 3469

Labour Weekly
Transport House
Smith Square
London SW1
tel: 01-834 9434

The Leveller
57 Caledonian Road
London N1
tel: 01-278 0146

Marxism Today
16 King Street
London WC2
tel: 01-836 2151

Militant
Mentmore Works
1 Mentmore Terrace
London E8
tel: 01-986 3828

Morning Star
(see national newspaper list)

Newsline
(see national newspaper list)

Peace News
8 Elm Avenue
Nottingham
tel: 0602 53857

Freedom
84b Whitechapel High Street
London E1
tel: 01-247 9249

Hibernia
206 Pearse Street
Dublin 2

Rebecca
15 Windsor Esplanade
Docks
Cardiff

Socialist Challenge
328 Upper Street
London N1
tel: 01-359 8180

Socialist Worker
PO Box 82
London E2
tel: 01-739 9043

Spare Rib
27 Clerkenwell Close
London EC1
tel: 01-253 9792

Peoples News Service
(alternative news agency)
Oxford House
Derbyshire Street
London E2
tel: 01-739 9093 (extension 7)

Tribune
24 St John Street
London EC1
tel: 01-253 2994

Undercurrents
27 Clerkenwell Close
London EC1
tel: 01-253 7303

The Chartist
60 Loughborough Road
London SW9

Community newspapers

This is a strictly non-exhaustive list, as commmunity newspapers tend to have a spasmodic existence; nor does it include the many papers or magazines orientated towards a single issue – e.g. tenants' newspapers, anti-racist magazines.

Birmingham Broadside
173 Lozells Road
Birmingham B19 1HS
tel: 021-554 3295

Brighton Voice
7 Victoria Road
Brighton
tel: 0273 27878

Bristol Voice
46 Richmond Road
Bristol 6
tel: 0272 40491

Burnley Voice
c/o 28 Scott Park Road
Burnley
Lancs
tel: 0282 34142

Exeter Flying Post
1 Parliament Street
Exeter
tel: 0392 70424

Islington Gutter Press
2 St Pauls Road
London N1
tel: 01-226 0580

Leeds Other Paper
30 Blenheim Terrace
Leeds 2
tel: 0532 42351

New Manchester Review
Waterloo Place
182 Oxford Road
Manchester 13
tel: 061-273 5636

Rochdale Alternative Press
230 Spotland Road
Rochdale
Lancs
tel: 0706 44981

Sheffield Free Press
c/o 341 Glossop Road
Sheffield 10
tel: 0742 737722

York Free Press
c/o York Community Books
73 Walmgate
York
tel: 0904 37355

Ethnic minority press

Bengali

Banglar Dak (weekly)
56 Methuen Road
Edgware
Middlesex
tel: 01-952 2155

Bangladesh (weekly)
48 Wilberforce Road
London N4
tel: 01-226 9626

Janomot
80 Hearnville Road
London SW12
tel: 01-673 8114

English

The Asian (monthly)
101 Praed Street
London W2

Jamaican Weekly Gleaner (weekly)
International Press Centre
Suite 511
76 Shoe Lane
London EC4
tel: 01-353 1604

India Weekly (weekly)
Wheatsheaf House
4 Carmelite House
London EC4
tel: 01-353 9091

The Afro-Caribbean Weekly Post
(weekly)
5 Grantham Road
London SW9
tel: 01-737 2474

Race Today (monthly)
74 Shakespeare Road
London SE24
tel: 01-737 2268

West Indian World (weekly)
111 Mathias Road
London N16
tel: 01-254 9602

Greek

To Vema (weekly)
268 Kingsland Road
London E8
tel: 01-249 2867

Parikiaki Haravghi
48a Artillery Lane
London E1
tel: 01-247 8574

Embros
79 Clarence Gate Gardens
London NW1
tel: 01-262 2830

Gujarati

Garavi Gujarat (weekly)
1/2 Silex Street
London SE1
tel: 01-261 1527

Gujarat Samachar (weekly)
303b Chiswick High Road
London W4
tel: 01-994 6655

Navjeevan
1 Lancelot Parade
Lancelot Road
Wembley
Middlesex
tel: 01-903 9199

Hindi

Amar Deep (weekly)
2 Chepstow Road
London W7
tel: 01-572 0980

Navin Weekly (weekly)
307a Northend Road
London W14
tel: 01-385 8966

Punjabi

Desperdes
8 The Crescent
Southall
Middlesex

Punjab Times
30 Featherstone Road
Southall
Middlesex
tel: 01-571 5102

Turkish

Isci Postasi (Workers News)
(fortnightly)
129 Newington Green Road
London N1
tel: 01-359 2023

Tamil

London Murasu (monthly)
8 Ashen Grove
London SW19
tel: 01-946 3374

Urdu

Aaj (weekly)
1a George Street
Southall
Middlesex
tel: 01-574 4309

Azad
20–22 York Way
London N1
tel: 01-278 8818

Daily Jang
52 Hoxton Square
London N1
tel: 01-739 1698

Daily Millat
333 Goswell Road
London EC1
tel: 01-837 9267

Mahriq (weekly)
82 Caledonian Road
London N1
tel: 01-837 6924

Milap (weekly)
307a Northend Road
London W14
tel: 01-385 8966

Voice of Kashmir (monthly)
438 Alum Rock Road
Birmingham 8
tel: 021-328 2467

Monthly trade-union journals

Actors' Equity Association,
British

Equity
8 Harley Street,
London W1N 2AB
tel: 01-636 6367

Agricultural and Allied Workers,
National Union of

Landworker
Headland House,
308–312 Gray's Inn Road,
London WC1X 8DS
tel: 01-278 7801

Bakers' Food and Allied Workers

Food Worker
Stanborough House,
Great North Road,
Stanborough,
Welwyn Garden City
Herts AL8 7TA
tel: 30 60150

Bank Employees, National
Union of

NUBE News
Sheffield House,
Portsmouth Road,
Esher,
Surrey KT10 9BH
tel.: 78 66624

Broadcasting Staff, Association of

Broadcast
King's Court,
2–16 Goodge Street,
London W1P 2AE
tel: 01-637 1261

Cinematograph, Television and Allied Technicians, Association of
Film and TV Technician
2 Soho Square,
London W1V 6DD
tel: 01-437 8506

Civil and Public Services Association
Red Tape
215 Balham High Road,
London SW17 7BQ
tel: 01-672 1299

Civil and Public Servants, Society of
Opinion
124–126 Southwark Street,
London SE1 0TU
tel: 01-928 9671

Civil Service Union
The Whip
14–21 Hatton Wall,
London EC1 8JP
tel: 01-242 2991

Construction, Allied Trades and Technicians Union of
Viewpoint
UCATT House,
177 Abbeville Road,
London SW4 9RL
tel: 01-622 2442

Engineers and Managers Association
Electrical Power Engineer
Station House,
Fox Lane North,
Chertsey,
Surrey KT16 9HW
tel: 093 28 64131

AUEW Construction Section
Construction Worker
Construction House,
190 Cedars Road,
Clapham,
London SW4 0PP
tel: 01-622 4451

AUEW Engineering Section
AUEW Journal
110 Peckham Road,
London SE15
tel: 01-703 4231

AUEW Technical, Administrative and Supervisory Section
TASS Journal
Onslow Hall,
Little Green,
Richmond,
Surrey
tel: 01-948 2271

Fire Brigades Union
Firefighter
Bradley House,
Fulham High Street,
London SW6 3JN
tel: 01-736 2157

Furniture, Timber and Allied Trades Union
FTAT Record
'Fairfields',
Roe Green,
London NW9
tel: 01-204 0273

General and Municipal Workers, National Union of
GMWU Journal
Thorne House,
Ruxley Ridge,
Claygate, Esher
Surrey KT10 0TL
tel: 78 62081

Graphical and Allied Trades, Society of
SOGAT Journal
274–288 London Road,
Hadleigh, Benfleet,
Essex SS7 2DE
tel: 0702 553131

Graphical Association, National
Print
Graphic House,
63–67 Bromham Road,
Bedford MK10 2AG
tel: 0234 51521

Greater London Council Staff
Association
London Town
Room 443A,
County Hall,
London SE1 7PB
tel: 01-633 5927

Health Services Employees,
Confederation of
Health Services
Glen House,
High Street,
Banstead, Surrey
tel: 25 53322

Health Visitors' Association
Health Visitor
36 Eccleston Square,
London SW1V 1PF
tel: 01-834 9523

Inland Revenue Staff Federation
Taxes
7 St George's Square,
London SW1V 2HY
tel: 01-834 8254

Iron and Steel Trades'
Confederation
Man and Metal
Swinton House,
324 Gray's Inn Road,
London WC1
tel: 01-837 6691

Journalists, National Union of
Journalist
314 Gray's Inn Road,
London WC1X 8DP
tel: 01-278 7916

Lithographic Artists, Designers,
Engravers and Process Workers,
Society of
SLADE Journal
Slade House,
155 Clapham Common
South Side,
London SW4 9DF
tel: 01-720 7551

Locomotive Engineers and
Firemen, Associated Society of
Locomotive Journal
9 Arkwright Road,
Hampstead,
London NW3 6AB
tel: 01-435 2160

Merchant Navy and Air Line
Officers' Association
The Telegraph
Oceanair House,
750–760 High Road,
Leytonstone,
London E11 3BB
tel: 01-989 6677

Mineworkers', National Union of
The Miner
222 Euston Road,
London NW1 2BX
tel: 01-387 7631

National and Local Government
Officers' Association
Public Service
1 Mabledon Place,
London WC1H 94J
tel: 01-388 2366

Patternmakers and Allied
Craftsmen, Association of
Patternmaker
15 Cleve Road,
West Hampstead,
London NW6 1YA
tel: 01-624 7085

Post Office Engineering Union
POEU Journal
Greystoke House,
150 Brunswick Road,
London W5 1AW
tel: 01-998 2981

Post Office Workers, Union of
The Post
UPW House,
Crescent Lane,
Clapham Common,
London SW4 9RN
tel: 01-622 9977

Printers, Graphical and Media
Personnel, National Society of
Operative
Journal and Graphic Review
Caxton House,
13/16 Borough Road,
London SE1 0AL
tel: 01-928 1481

Prison Officers' Association
Prison Officers' Magazine
245 Church Street,
London N9 9HW
tel: 01-807 3383

Professional Civil Servants,
Institution of
State Service
3/7 Northumberland Street
London WC2N 5BS
tel: 01-930 9755

Public Employees, National Union
of
Public Employees
Civic House,
Aberdeen Terrace,
London SE3 0QY
tel: 01-852 2842

Professional Executive, Clerical
and Computer Staff, Association of
APEX
22 Worple Road,
London SW19
tel: 01-947 3131

Railwaymen, National Union of
Transport Review
205 Euston Road,
London NW1 2BL
tel: 01-387 4771

Schoolmasters and Union of
Women Teachers, National
Association of
Schoolmaster and Career Teacher
Swan Court,
Waterhouse Street,
Hemel Hempstead,
Herts
tel: 0442 2971/4

Scientific, Technical and
Managerial Staffs, Association of
ASTMS Journal
10–26a Jamestown Road,
London NW10 7DT
tel: 01-267 4422

Seamen, National Union of
Seamen
Maritime House,
Old Town,
Clapham,
London SW4 0JP
tel: 01-622 5581

Sheet Metal Workers,
Coppersmiths, Heating and
Domestic Engineers, National
Union of
The Journal
75–77 West Heath Road,
London NW3 7TL
tel: 01-455 0053

Shop, Distributive and Allied
Workers, Union of
Dawn
'Oakley',
188 Wilmslow Road,
Fallowfield
Manchester, M14 6LJ
tel: 061-224 2804

Tailors and Garment Workers,
National Union of

Garment Worker
Radlett House,
West Hill,
Aspley Guise,
Milton Keynes, MK17 8DT
tel: 0908 583099

Teachers, National Union of

The Teacher
Hamilton House,
Mabledon Place,
London WC1H 9BD
tel: 01-387 2442

Teachers in Further and Higher
Education, National Association
of

NATFHE Journal
Hamilton House,
Mabledon Place,
London WC1H 9BH
tel: 01-387 6806

Theatrical, Television and Kine
Employees, National Association
of

NATTKE Newsletter
155 Kennington Park Road,
London SE11 4JU
tel: 01-735 9068

Transport and General Workers'
Union

TGWU Record
Transport House,
Smith Square,
London SW1P 3JB
tel: 01-828 7788

Transport Salaried Staffs'
Association

Transport Salaried Staff Journal
Walkden House,
10 Melton Street,
London NW1 2ET
tel: 01-387 2101

University Teachers, Association
of

University Teachers Bulletin
United House,
1 Pembridge Road,
London, W11 3HJ
tel: 01-221 4370

Writers' Guild of Great Britain,

Writers' News
430 Edgware Road,
London W2 1EH
tel: 01-723 8074

Other useful addresses

Chairman Complaints Committee
BBC
Broadcasting House
Portland Place
London W1
tel: 01-580 4468

Chairman/Complaints Committee
Independent Broadcasting
Authority
70 Brompton Road
London SW3
tel: 01-584 7011

The Press Council
1 Salisbury Square
London EC4
tel: 01-353 1248

National Union of Journalists
Acorn House
314–20 Grays Inn Road
London WC1
tel: 01-278 7916

Index